LIBRARY PROGRAMS ONLINE

Possibilities and Practicalities of Web Conferencing

Thomas A. Peters

LIBRARIES UNLIMITED

An Imprint of ABC-CLIO, LLC

A B C ☙ C L I O

Santa Barbara, California • Denver, Colorado • Oxford, England

Library of Congress Cataloging-in-Publication Data

Peters, Thomas A., 1957–
   Library programs online : possibilities and practicalities of Web conferencing /
   Thomas A. Peters.
      p. cm.
   Includes bibliographical references and index.
   ISBN 978–1–59158–349–3 (acid-free paper)
1. Computer conferencing—Library applications. 2. Online Programming for All Libraries
(Program) I. Title.
Z674.75.W67P48   2009
004.67′8—dc22   2009027036

13 12 11 10 9   1 2 3 4 5

This book is also available on the World Wide Web as an eBook.
Visit www.abc-clio.com for details.

ABC-CLIO, LLC
130 Cremona Drive, P.O. Box 1911
Santa Barbara, California 93116-1911

This book is printed on acid-free paper ∞

Manufactured in the United States of America

To my wife, Vicki

Contents

Acknowledgments

Many people have provided support during the writing of this book. I especially wish to thank my colleague and friend, Lori Bell, who got me involved in online programming at the right time. My editor at Libraries Unlimited, Barbara Ittner, has been very encouraging and unbelievably patient. I also appreciate the loving support of my wife, Vicki, whose first question when she sees me at the computer in my home office has become, "Are you currently involved in an online event?" Even our four children have learned to tone down their uproar when they see and hear Dad talking into that funny looking PC microphone.

Preface

This book is the direct reflection of the many experiences I have had in the past six years managing a collaborative online programming initiative called OPAL: Online Programs for All. OPAL is a collaborative Web conferencing and online public programming service begun by the Mid-Illinois Talking Book Center in the summer of 2003 as a way to offer online book discussions and other types of programs to blind and visually impaired patrons, who, although generally quite mobile, did not frequently visit the Center. Most libraries for the blind and physically handicapped, as they are generically known, are not designed to handle lots of in-person services. The telephone, online communication, and—most recently—encounters in virtual worlds are the primary channels of communication. OPAL has since grown to encompass all types of libraries on three continents (primarily North America), with even a few non-library organizational members.

Back in the summer of 2003 I met with Lori Bell, who was then serving as the Director of the Mid-Illinois Talking Book Center. She approached me about conducting some online book discussions and interviews primarily for library patrons who were blind or visually impaired. Neither Lori nor I could have imagined that from that little seed would grow such an exciting new endeavor of online public programming for libraries.

The initial start-up phase of this new endeavor was particularly challenging. Although Web conferencing systems had been in existence for years, it was a new sphere of experience for me. I never had used Web conferencing software before, nor had I even used voice-over-Internet Protocol (VoIP) in any context before, so I needed to purchase a microphone to use with my computer. I distinctly remember purchasing the least expensive PC microphone I could find—less than $10, including sales tax—thinking that, if this entire project flopped I wouldn't be out that much money.

During the first online interview I conducted, I was using a dial-up connection to the Internet that caused some logistical problems. The connection was so slow that the audio packets usually arrived all broken up and delayed. During some points in the interview I had to resort to asking the next question before I received the previous response. I would simply guess how the interviewee had responded and then ask another question that hopefully was not redundant, incoherent, or a complete non sequitur.

But after hundreds of online events and meetings, and many valuable lessons learned, as well as improvements in technology, my anxiety level has subsided. Now having broadband Internet service has become as essential for the Web conferences as food, clothing, and shelter is for me. But I still am using that inexpensive microphone.

For the past six years I have had the pleasure of serving as the day-to-day coordinator of the OPAL collaborative online programming service. Although I hope this book proves useful to a wide variety of librarians in all types of libraries, I have imagined that I am writing to a newly hired or appointed manager of an emerging online programming service. As such, I have tried to identify and organize the issues, the successes, and the errors that I have observed—and made—thus far in my Web conferencing experience.

Although I have written this book with an ideal reader in mind—another coordinator of an online programming service—it should be useful to a variety of individuals, groups, and organizations. People in public libraries responsible for adult and children's programming are the primary audience. Associate directors for public services in public libraries also may be interested in this innovative and tech-savvy programming effort. Staff members at state libraries, library consortia, library systems, and library associations may find something of interest and use here as well. Additionally, *Library Programs Online* may appeal to some academic librarians, especially those at institutions who really try to reach out to the citizens of the local community, the region, the state, and so on.

In this era of high transportation costs, busy schedules, and tight budgets, Web conferencing software offers another benefit to every library administrator—reducing the cost of public programs, meetings, professional development workshops, and other group events. Beneath the visible part of the online programming iceberg lies a vast array of intra- and interorganizational uses to make communications in and between libraries as efficient and effective as possible.

Library consortia administrators and staff may see in this topic a new way to leverage the power of collaboration. OPAL itself certainly has proven to be a successful, loosely organized collaborative involving a wide variety of libraries and library-related organizations. Library associations and other organizations serving libraries should see in online programming a great way to complement—not necessarily supplant—in-person conferences, workshops, and meetings. Furthermore, *Library Programs Online* may be adopted as supplemental reading for courses in public services, adult and children's programming, and perhaps even digital library development, now that many digital libraries are expanding their visions beyond digitized content and metadata to full-scale online services.

this book we occasionally mention and briefly examine how Web conferencing systems are being used by one or two individuals, the primary focus of this book is on the use of Web conferencing systems by groups to hold live online group gatherings, also known as group events and meetings, especially live online events offered to the general public.

Sometimes these live online programs are designed for the general public. Lectures, book discussions, workshops, concerts, and other types of public programs have been offered in physical libraries for years. These programs are used to teach, highlight library collections and services, and even delight the group members who attend. Other library programs are offered primarily for library and information science professionals. Staff development programs about Library 2.0 tools (blogs, wikis, podcasts, etc. [see below]) and other information technology topics are currently very popular.

A blog, a shortened form of the word weblog is a series of short essays, reports, commentaries and other material usually written by an individual, posted to a Web site, and listed in reverse chronological order. A wiki, based on the Hawaiian word for fast, is a collaborative Web site at which a group of authorized editors (potentially everyone in the world) can edit and add to the content in the wiki. A podcast, a mashup of the words iPod and broadcast, is a series of audio and/or video files that are released as feeds over a period of time using one or more web syndication methods, such as RSS (really simple syndication).

When considered in the context of the library's overall mission, vision, and service cluster, however, live events for groups may be closer to the perimeter than to the center of a library's mission. In many—if not most—real-world libraries, as well as in many digital libraries, collections remain at the center of the library's focus and investment of resources. Metadata services include any type of service involving the creation, organization, distribution, or other value-adding service related to metadata—data about data. Examples of metadata include the data included in library catalog records and the tags assigned to digital photos. Services that directly relate to the collections (such as metadata services) and to people finding information in the collections (such as reference services) often more closely relate to the library's mission than peripheral services such as events and exhibits.

In addition, for many libraries, serving groups as groups often takes a subtle back seat to serving individual library users. In an article I wrote for *Smart Libraries Newsletter* entitled "The End of the Romantic Library?" (July 2007), I dubbed libraries that serve primarily individuals "Romantic Libraries." Until the first decade of the present century, most libraries were Romantic libraries.

"Romanticism put the individual self on a pedestal," I said in the article. "The self, perhaps in direct response to its interaction with elemental natural forces (or at least the contemplation of those forces), was the source of all creativity. Individual experience was the main thing. Groups and group behavior did not count for much. Crowded fields of daffodils were more interesting to William Wordsworth than crowds of people. Romantic poets did not write much about crowded places and the value of crowds, let alone the 'wisdom of crowds,' which probably would have been dismissed by romantic poets and philosophers as an absurd phrase."

In contrast, live online programming is primarily about public programs (lectures, discussions, and so on) and staff development opportunities for groups. Public programming and staff development, although essential, are not at the core of the missions of most traditional libraries.

Even within the realm of "third place" public services, public events (online or in-person) do not currently rate very high in the pecking order. In most libraries, reference service is considered a more essential public service and worthy of more time, money, and other organizational resources than public information forums. In academic libraries and elsewhere, bibliographic instruction would usually trump public events. Whether in-person or online, public events may be the runt of the public services litter.

Nonetheless, do not underestimate the future of online public events, especially in the light of the recent rapid rise in the cost of transportation. The value of public programming in the overall mission and goals structure of a particular library or library-related organization may rise as more libraries develop a presence in the massive multi-user virtual environments (MUVEs) (http://en.wikipedia.org/wiki/Muve) such as Second Life, Active Worlds, and There.com. The early experiences of the worldwide team of volunteer librarian-avatars of the Alliance Second Life Library project seem to indicate that exhibits and live online public events may play a much larger role in libraries in virtual environments than it does for libraries in the real world (*A Report on the First Year of Operation of the Alliance Second Life Library 2.0 Project*, also known as the Alliance Information Archipelago, www.alliancelibrarysystem.com/pdf/07sllreport.pdf).

The idea of social networks, specifically professional networking, in the sense of connecting and communicating with colleagues, has been around for decades. The *Wikipedia* article on social networking traces the first instance of the phrase back to 1954 by J. A. Barnes in a study of a Norwegian island parish. Within the past few years, the concept of online social networking using Web 2.0 tools and virtual environments has become all the rage.

The purpose of *Library Programs Online* is to define, describe, and sway the future development of the emerging field within librarianship involved in developing and sustaining an online library programming service. Online library programming is defined as public programs (lectures, demonstrations, interviews, book discussions, story hours, and more) that are delivered in real time (that is, live) primarily over the Web, utilizing a variety of interactive communication tools, including VoIP (voice-over-Internet Protocol—a cluster of standards and technologies that enable voice communication to be transmitted over networks that use the Internet Protocol), text chatting (a form of communicating where two or more people type short, informal utterances back and forth, often displayed sequentially in a text chat window), and co-browsing (enabling two or more people in the same online environment to browse to the same locations on the Web at approximately the same time). Although distance education programs—that allow instructors and students to teach and learn in a common space without being in the same physical location (Learning Management Systems such as WebCT and Moodle often are used to manage and deliver distance education programs)—in higher education, corporate and governmental training efforts, and other sectors of society have developed and deployed similar online programming systems and services, this book focuses on how libraries (public, academic, school, and special) and library-related organizations (library associations, consortia, library and IT publishers, vendors, and so on) can and are developing online programs for library users and librarians.

A distinction is being made here between live *in-person* library programs that are offered in bricks-and-mortar libraries, live *online* library programs that are offered on the Web using various systems and technologies, and live *in-world* library programs that are offered in virtual worlds. While live library programs in any venue or environment share some common characteristics, challenges, and opportunities, each specific environment adds its own set of nuances and wrinkles.

The technology that drives live online events is generally called Web conferencing software. (See http://en.wikipedia.org/wiki/Web_conferencing.)

Library Programs Online explores how libraries and library-related organizations are using and could use Web conferencing systems for a wide range of live group events, prerecorded programs and podcasts, and previously recorded archived events.

SYNCHRONOUS (LIVE) AND ASYNCHRONOUS (DELAYED) GROUP COMMUNICATION

A classic distinction is often invoked between synchronous (live) group communication and asynchronous (delayed) group communication. A conference call, for example, is synchronous, while a correspondence course is asynchronous. The focus of this book is on synchronous group communication using Web conferencing software, but we will turn our attention as appropriate to asynchronous group communication.

Can real-time, synchronous group communication be tightly defined? After all, there always is a little time delay between when a message is sent and when it is received. When I gesture to someone across a distance, it takes a fraction of a second for the light to travel from my gesturing arm to the retinas of the eyes of the other members of my group. If I utter an audible communication, it takes even longer for the sound to travel. The audio signal delivered via Web conferencing software often experiences some network delays from a fraction of a second to several seconds.

Nevertheless, for the purposes of this book we consider live online events delivered via Web conferencing software to be one type of synchronous group communication. The fact that live online events can be recorded, archived, and podcast, and thus turned into a form of asynchronous communication, does not diminish their worth and impact as live online events.

FIVE BASIC REAL-TIME GROUP COMMUNICATION OPTIONS

Humans are gregarious creatures. We love to get together in groups—for safety, learning, and enjoyment. When groups convene, they need the means and modes of communication. If a group of three or more humans wants to communicate in real-time, the group must select a mode of communication that supports real-time communication. Five basic types of synchronous group communication currently exist: in-person, telephone conference calls, video conferencing, online, and in-world.

In-Person, or Face-to-Face Communication

The most ancient mode of communicating, and probably still the most popular, is in-person communication. The group gets together. The iconic image here is of a group of people sitting around a conference table holding a meeting. That is what groups have been doing since before recorded human history, although the conference table was likely a fire. In all languages, a plethora of names have arisen to describe and differentiate various types of live, in-person group gatherings. In English, the group get-together may be called a meeting, workshop, class, seminar, conference, symposium, confab, happening, rave, or something else; but all of these things fall into the general category of a real-time, in-person group communication.

Transportation time and costs need to be factored into the planning for any in-person meeting, even if all the attendees work in the same building. If the individual members of the group are in close geographic proximity prior to the convening of the in-person, real-time meeting, the transportation costs to get to and from the meeting are minimal.

The big advantage of in-person, real-time group communication is that the full spectra of both verbal and nonverbal communication are available to each member of the group. Words, voice inflection, facial expressions, hand gestures, body language, dress and adornment, and every other possible way to communicate are available and viable means of communication. We have not yet devised another means of group real-time, in-person communication that meets or exceeds the good old in-person meeting in terms of richness and complexity.

All real-time group communication develops over time. One common complaint about many instances of group real-time communication is that the communication process takes too long. Interminable meetings, for example, can affect group morale and effectiveness. When some individual or group complains that a meeting took too long, what they really seem to be saying is that their return on investment of time and attention in attending the meeting was not good—the benefits of attending the meeting did not off-set the time and attention spent attending (and traveling to and from) the meeting.

However, for any real-time, in-person group gathering that lasts more than, say, an hour, the opportunity for group breaks and group meals adds another set of advantages for an in-person meeting. During these breaks people get to chat about topics related and unrelated to the meeting agenda and purpose. Even during relatively short meetings (yes, brief meetings do occur occasionally), the pre-meeting and post-meeting conversations may help improve the return-on-investment ratio for the attendees. The people attending the meeting get to renew acquaintances, meet new people, share ideas, gossip, and so forth. The value of these "extracurricular" communications on the attendees' estimate of the overall value of attending the live in-person event should not be underestimated.

Although real-time, in-person group communication continues to be the most popular mode or channel of group communication, with no contender on the horizon to seriously challenge its long reign, this mode of communication does have its downsides. Everyone has to agree to the start and end time. Morning people and afternoon people must reach some common agreement. If people are coming from different time zones to attend a live, in-person meeting, diurnal disruptions in individual schedules and jet lag can affect the group's overall effectiveness: you could take an overnight transatlantic flight to attend a morning meeting in London, but you may not be full of vim and vigor during the in-person meeting.

Further, any disruption to an individual engaged in the in-person group communication tends to disrupt the entire communication. The incoming cell phone call is a glaring, unpleasant example of how an interruption intended to draw away the attention of one individual often affects negatively, if only momentarily, the entire group's communication process. When attending a live, in-person event, it can be difficult to separate and contain communication intended for one individual participant.

Real-time, in-person group communication also forces the participants to enter the same ambient environment—the meeting space. It is difficult—perhaps impossible—to find a room temperature that will be optimal to every individual attending the in-person event. Someone always is going to be too warm or too cool. The lighting may be too bright or too low for some, too. The chairs may not be comfortable for many or most of the attendees. If refreshments or meals are to be served during the meeting, the various dietary preferences and restrictions of the individuals attending the meeting must be taken into consideration. In general, during most in-person, real-time communications, certain modes of dress, decorum, and deportment are expected of all attendees. Therefore, in-person group events perforce require the normalization and compromise of various comfort levels.

In this era of continually rising transportation costs, traveling to and from an in-person, real-time group communication often is perceived as the biggest downside to this mode of live communication. Unless all attending the group meeting work in the same building, the costs in time and expense to attend will not be insignificant. The cost to attend may actually prevent some people who want to or should be in attendance to either skip the meeting altogether or choose another communication channel.

Telephone Conference Calls

For millennia, in-person group communication was the only real-time communication option. If you wanted to communicate with two or more people in any other way, you had to resort to asynchronous communication. Letters served well as an asynchronous substitute for an in-person meeting, but exchanging letters is not really the same as meeting in person. Early forms of visually based communication among a group across relative long distances, such as semaphore signals sent between a group of ships at sea, are the exception that proves the rule.

Throughout the twentieth and twenty-first centuries, viable alternatives to the in-person mode of real-time group communication have emerged. The telephone conference call is one example. Although much of the richness of the in-person communication is unavailable or lost to the aural-only telephone conference call channel, a conference call does have the distinct advantage of reducing travel costs to nil.

Telephone conference calls generally are less expensive than in-person meetings. The direct cost of having a telephone conference call must be borne either by the individual or organization that "called" the meeting, or be distributed across everyone who is participating in the conference call. Conference calls tend to be used more for meetings of working groups and professional colleagues than for the delivery of public events such as lectures, workshops, and book discussions.

A telephone conference call avoids the necessity of a shared ambient environment. Each individual participating in the call may have some control over his or her local temperature setting, lighting level, and the like. A conference call also relaxes some of the dress, decorum, and deportment restrictions of an in-person meeting. You can even put your feet on the table if you want or mute your audio input and work on other things (or eat your lunch) while listening in on a telephone conference call group communication without worrying that you will offend another attendee.

On the downside, sharing documents, having private side-conversations, and other aspects of in-person meetings, usually are difficult or impossible during the typical telephone conference call. We can safely conclude, then, that online meetings are better than conference calls, for two basic reasons. First, conference calls are all about voice communication; they are all talk and only talk. If you want the conference call attendees to examine a Web site or other digital document together, the best you can do is announce the URL that everyone is supposed to visit (and hope that everyone is in front of an Internet-connected computer) or send out the URL before the actual conference call. With online events it is much easier to co-browse and examine and discuss visual information. Second, online meetings are generally less expensive than conference calls.

Video Conferencing

Video conferencing was the third basic mode of real-time group communication to emerge. It has been around in various forms for over 40 years and is based and built on closed circuit television communications technology, such as Vtel and Polycom. Some libraries and library systems invested rather heavily in these types of systems.

The advantage of these types of meeting systems is that the video and voice are integrated, and the cost of television monitors continues to drop as the sizes of the screens increases. Most of the technological components of video conferencing systems are mature and reliable.

The biggest downside of most teleconferencing systems is that the points of participation usually are limited. Participants may need to travel a considerable distance just to get to the nearest participation point. Having to travel only 25 miles rather than 100 miles to attend a meeting is good, but it still involves some travel time and, perhaps more importantly, being away from your desk where multitasking can occur during lulls in the video conferencing interaction.

State libraries, consortia, and regional systems use video conferencing systems. According to a report by Higgs-Horwell and Schwelik (2007), video conferencing systems have been used successfully by INFOhio (www.infohio.org) to provide professional development seminars for Ohio school librarians.

Although systems like VTel and Polycom may seem a little antiquated as legacy systems now, system developments and improvements continue to be made. For example, Hewlett-Packard has developed a next-generation video conferencing system called Halo Collaboration Suites. HP has already installed dozens of Halo rooms for corporate clients such as Dreamworks Animation. They hope to offer Halo rooms for personal use within five years (Anonymous 2008).

Cisco and other companies have developed what they call telepresence technologies, described by Dickinson (2007) as "a video collaboration technology that is supposed to deliver high-definition images and stereophonic sound with enough realism to enable useful collaboration." The telepresence technology uses high-definition television screens and cameras, using camera angles that make it seem as if everyone is sitting right across from everyone else. Often the presentation slides and other non-visage-based information are presented on a separate monitor. Of course, in these early years of telepresence technology, the costs remain high—well into six figures to outfit two or more rooms with the specialized equipment.

Another problem with these early versions of telepresence systems is they often are built on proprietary platforms that are incompatible with other telepresence systems. However, gains are being made. In mid-2007 a small technology company called Teliris launched a product called Telepresence Gateway, which the company claims is the first product to support interoperability between different telepresence platforms. Telepresence Gateway also reportedly works with traditional video conferencing systems from companies such as Polycom, as well as with Web conferencing systems such as WebEx from Cisco and LiveMeeting from Microsoft (Dickinson 2007).

Web Conferencing

Web conferencing software was developed in the late twentieth century as another mode or option for real-time group communication. The use of Web conferencing software by libraries and library-related groups and individuals is the primary focus of *Library Programs Online*. One way to understand Web conferencing in the context of the five fundamental modes of live group communication is that it offers a means of communication that approaches the richness and complexity of in-person communication at a fraction of the cost of an in-person gathering and as such it is perceived by many as being better than telephone conferencing since it offers voice-over-IP, text chatting, co-browsing, and document sharing.

We should note that over the years other Internet-based technologies, such as text-chatting software, have added features that almost approximate Web conferencing software. The list of Web conferencing software on the "think of it" Web site is broken down into various categories, such as screen sharing software, instant messaging services, chat room software, remote PC access software, live customer sales and support systems, and more (http://thinkofit.com/webconf/realtime.htm).

Live In-World Group Communication in Virtual Worlds

One of the more interesting recent modes of real-time group communication occurs in virtual worlds such as Second Life (http://secondlife.com).

Groups convene in Second Life as a way to approximate the three-dimensional significance of real-time, in-person gatherings. Virtual worlds such as Second Life consist of persistent three-dimensional online environments in which the residents, known as avatars, can socialize, share information and experiences, learn formally and informally, and have fun. Virtual worlds generally are not considered online games, because, like real life, the "rules" of behavior usually are fluid and inexplicit.

As we move farther into the twenty-first century, virtual world meetings may become more popular and prevalent, perhaps at the expense of Web conferencing gatherings. In general, it will be interesting to watch the jockeying for market share that occurs between these five modes of group communication in the coming years and decades. Perhaps in-person meetings that require travel will become very expensive and precious. In-world meetings in virtual worlds may gain market share as the best available alternative to in-person events. Telephone conference calls may lose market share, and Web conferencing may gain market share. Telepresence group meetings may be the dark horse in this race. Several factors will influence how and why market shares will increase and decrease over time. The monetary cost to start and maintain each mode of communication will be a contributing factor, of course, as will the "cognitive cost" to learn and use the software programs that support each mode of real-time group communication. The effectiveness and ease of the group communication resulting from each mode will be a determining factor as well.

During these early years of group communication and collaboration in virtual worlds, the ability to share and interact with documents, even lowly presentation slides, can be difficult or unsatisfactory. The avatars who meet in these virtual worlds often like to sit around conference tables or in virtual lecture halls. Different types of group meeting venues, however, that foster group interaction in inventive ways, are beginning to appear in virtual worlds. Recording and archiving in-world group events can be difficult or easy, depending on your level of technical proficiency with the recording software and tools. Machinima—films made of activities in three-dimensional virtual worlds—of group events in Second Life, for example, are showing up with increasing frequency in video sharing resources such as YouTube (www.youtube.com).

Other Uncategorized Modes of Real-Time Group Communication

The previous five categories or modes of live (synchronous) group communication are not discrete, immutable, and ironclad. They combine, morph, and merge in interesting ways. As mentioned earlier, instant messaging (IM) services on the Web, for example, are taking on many of the features and functionalities of Web conferencing software, and two or more modes of live group communication can be combined to create a successful group event. I have participated in live group events where in-person, in-world, and online group communication modes all have been used together. Some people were in the same physical location, others were in Second Life, and others were in an OPAL (see next section) online Web conferencing room. It may sound chaotic and disorienting, but it actually works quite well.

Other real-time group communication options, many of which are difficult to categorize, have also emerged. The speed with which some groups instant message each other approaches a state of real-time group communication. Twittering (a popular micro-blogging blog where participants share "tweets" that are no more than 140 characters long [http://twitter.com]) and text-messaging on phones in general can be considered a form of near-real-time group communication. Many Web 2.0 social networking systems seem to be morphing and merging toward something that supports, virtually, live group communication and collaboration.

As the options for real-time group communication continue to multiply and evolve, groups are using multiple methods simultaneously to communicate. An early example of this was the meeting where some people attended in person while others participated via conference call. We can call these multi-modal meetings. It is not uncommon to see and experience meetings, workshops, and conferences where some people are in-person, some are in-world (i.e., attending in some virtual world), some are attending via Web conferencing, and some are attending via two or more modes. During the VCL MIG (Virtual Communities and Libraries Member Initiative Group) program at the ALA Annual Conference in Anaheim, some attendees and presenters were physically in the same room, other attendees participated from ALA Island in Second Life, where they could hear the audio and could text chat back to the presenters, and one of the leaders presented via Skype (a software service that enables Internet-based telephone calls) from northern California. Multi-modal group events may be increasingly important in the future, as event organizers offer various "modes" or "channels" to potential participants, allowing them to choose the channel that works best for them.

THREE-PRONGED APPROACH

Web conferencing systems, then, are just one arrow in a group or organization's quiver for communicating as a group. As an organization, during the course of a typical work day, a library may be involved in several in-person meetings, conference calls, Web conferencing-based meetings, in-world events in virtual words, and other forms of real-time group communication. Each library and library-related organization needs to decide which mix of meeting modes works best for its staff and clients. The "right mix" is a constantly moving target, too, as people explore and become acclimated to new meeting technologies, and as the technologies themselves improve and become easier to use and less expensive to implement.

How can we understand, then, and exploit the value (see definition above and in Chapter 10) of Web conferencing software in this complex mix of communication channels and opportunities? The value of Web conferencing software to a library or library-related organization depends in part on the value that organization places on the activities pursued with the software.

Although each library can decide how best to use its Web conferencing capacity to meet organizational needs and goals, a three-pronged approach seems to be emerging. Libraries and library-related organizations seem to be acquiring Web conferencing software to facilitate (1) private meetings, (2) professional and staff development opportunities, and (3) public programming. Although public programming may have a small but comfortable niche in the overall mission of many libraries, having efficient and effective internal communication and professional and staff development opportunities are generally regarded as more essential to the overall, long-term health and success of the organization.

To support these initiatives, progress in the development of live online events produced and delivered by libraries, library consortia, library associations, and other library-related organizations is accelerating. Following is a closer look at the three applications of online programming:

1. Public Programs
2. Training, Continuing Education, and Professional and Staff Development
3. Online Conferences

Let's examine how one collaborative library-based Web conferencing service has developed an array of online programs for library workers and the general public. OPAL (Online Programs for All) (www.opal-online.org) began as an initiative to offer live online public programs to blind and low-vision library users. For these users, the digital revolution and the acceptance of the notion of a library without walls was a tremendous boon, because it is difficult for them to physically visit and use a bricks-and-mortar library. Accessing digital information resources on the Web using screen reader software is much easier and more fruitful for this population than navigating through the real world to find and use information resources and information services that are also available on the Internet. Many of these users are very computer literate and were into online social networking long before it became "cool."

In 2003 OPAL began to offer book discussions and other public programs to this service population, but its de facto mission soon expanded. Mirroring the market's changes, OPAL had evolved into a three-pronged program by late 2005.

First, the mainstay of the program continued to be the "fully public" online programs that were available to library users worldwide. (Although most attendees of OPAL events are located in the United States, to date attendees from every continent except Antarctica have participated. By this time, we were pleased to learn that we had developed a worldwide audience for OPAL live online programs.) These fully public online programs remain free of charge and do not require registration. Anyone with access to an Internet-connected computer can attend. This is the visible tip of the OPAL online group communication iceberg.

The second prong has focused on live online continuing education and professional development opportunities for library staff members and librarians. These free, online opportunities for professional development and engagement have proven to be quite popular, often drawing between 25 and 150 attendees, with many more library staff members benefitting from the archived recordings of these sessions.

The OPAL team has begun the third prong by developing larger scale online events, such as full-day workshops and multi-day online conferences. In late July 2005 our initial experiment was launched in what we call the "Let's Go Library Expo" series of online conferences. In 2006 the Alliance Library System organized several one- and two-day conferences that were held, at the very least, both in-person in the real world as well as live online in OPAL. Participants could either travel to the conference location to participate in person, or they could attend online using the OPAL Web conferencing platform.

As described here, this three-pronged approach seems very neat and clean. In reality, however, the process is gloriously messy. Some of the best live online programs I have been involved in have been crossover or fused online events that attract both librarians and end-users—and several other key stakeholder groups in the information chain or loop, such as publishers, authors, and information technologists. One wonderful thing about live online programs is that people attend from many different locations and for many different reasons. Because text chatting is available to everyone who attends a live online event, they often use text chat to share their ideas and perspectives on the topic being discussed or presented.

At first glance, public online programs and staff development programs appear to be two sides of the same coin. However, online programs using Web conferencing software offer a unique opportunity for a common meeting space and online event experience where librarians, end-users, vendors, information technologists, authors, agents, and others in the information supply-usage circle meet to converse, share ideas and information, and collaborate on projects.

Although the emphasis is on online library programming intended for the general public, in-service staff training and professional development programs fall within the scope of this book as well. After all, programming geared toward library staff and librarians is important, too. Some of the best online programs attract "crossover crowds" such as librarians, library users, publishers, and technology people, which result in useful interactions. Several OPAL online sessions, like the "Virtual Worlds for Kids, Tweens and Teens" panel discussion held on January 25, 2008, have included participants from both the information industry and the library profession.

WHY SHOULD YOUR LIBRARY OR CONSORTIUM PROVIDE ONLINE PROGRAMS?

A great benefit to providing online programs is to meet your library patrons where they increasingly live and work—online. People are more likely to attend an online library program than an in-library public program for a number of reasons. There is no travel time involved, and no need to leave home or the office; many people are able to monitor an online event while attending to other tasks, important in this era in which multitasking seems to be firmly entrenched in the information-intensive population.

Furthermore, online programs make your library more competitive in the marketplace. Online public programming can extend your library's reach into the service population, grab the attention of some early adopters and opinion leaders in the community you serve, and convey to other libraries that your library is moving boldly into the digital future. Plus, because online programs are easily recorded and redistributed on demand, your library gets more bang for each buck it invests in its public programming outreach.

Looking to the future, online programs will only become more cost effective. The costs in dollars and time lost traveling to and from in-person live events are significant. For the foreseeable future, travel expenses probably will outpace the general rate of inflation. This burden is borne both by libraries as organizations and by library patrons. If S. R. Ranganathan—noted mathematician and librarian from India who developed the famous five laws of library science—were alive today, he would likely have exhorted us to save the time *and the money* of the user.

Libraries have to adhere to budgets just like corporations. Therefore, one shouldn't feel ashamed to use Web conferencing software, developed initially for the corporate world, to meet goals and advance service missions. Heck (2005) reports that a recent survey by the Travel Industry Association of America found that, of the business air travelers interviewed, nearly three out of four reported that they believed a Web conference meeting would be somewhat or much more efficient than traveling to meet face-to-face. Wouldn't the same hold true for your library programs and training sessions?

On the other hand, Web conferencing software is not a panacea and probably will not replace all face-to-face meetings. For many participants, Web conferencing beats face-to-face meetings on the efficiency measure, but not on the effectiveness measure. Only 37 percent of the interviewees in the travel survey thought online meetings would be more effective. Let's face it, with online meetings you often miss the little movements, facial expressions, glances, and gestures—what the philosopher Gottfried Leibniz called petite perceptions—that often provide subtle meaning to an in-person meeting, workshop, or conference.

There are other arguments for and against online programs, most of which are addressed in greater detail in Chapter 10, but for the time being, suffice it to say that we believe the advantages far outweigh the disadvantages.

DEFINITIONS OF WEB CONFERENCING AND ONLINE LIBRARY PROGRAMS

Wikipedia, the free online collaborative encyclopedia, defines Web conferencing this way: "Web conferencing is used to conduct live meetings or presentations via the Internet. In a web conference, each participant sits at his or her own computer and is connected to the other participants via the internet. This can be either a downloaded application on each of the attendee's computers or a web-based application where the attendees will simply enter a URL (Web site address) to enter the conference. . . . In the early years of the Internet, the term 'Web conferencing' was often used to describe a group discussion in a message board and therefore not live. The term has evolved to refer specifically to live or 'synchronous' meetings" (http://en.wikipedia.org/wiki/Web_conferencing, accessed March 14, 2009).

Web conferencing essentially is the use of the Internet to conduct a live online event (a meeting, presentation, workshop, conference, and so on) where people can communicate via one or more channels (such as, chat, voice-over-IP, and nonverbal communication via Web cams) and share information and documents via one or more channels (like synchronized browsing, presentation slides, application and desktop sharing, and whiteboarding [the online equivalent of writing on a white dry-erase board]).

Live online library programming, then, can be defined as the method by which libraries, library consortia, library systems, library associations, and other library-related organizations utilize the basic technologies and functionality of Web conferencing systems to offer live online events that may be of interest to library users, librarians, and other information professionals.

This is all relatively simple and straightforward, but there are several potentially interesting branches of Web conferencing usage. For example, most Web conferencing services offer a way to record live online events. These recordings can then be archived so that people who missed the live online event can enjoy it and gain value from it by watching and listening to the archived recording. A live online library programming service, then, can (and perhaps should) have recording and archiving components.

In addition, with some Web conferencing recording services it is possible to isolate and reuse the various components of a recorded live online event. For example, the audio recording of a live online event can be podcast. In that way, people could be listening to a presentation on their MP3 players and have little or no awareness that it originally was given as a live online event.

Even the audio portion of live online events can be delivered and broadcast in different ways. Some Web conferencing services offer an Internet radio broadcast option, whereby participants can listen to the live audio broadcast (with a few seconds' delay) of a live online event delivered through a standard Web browser software program, without having to install a special Web conferencing software client or entering some online room to listen to the live online event. Of course, their ability to access other communication and information sharing channels associated with the live online event, such as text chatting, co-browsing, and presentation slides, may be restricted or impossible, but for certain types of events the live audio stream is the main message. Some Web conferencing systems also offer the ability to transfer the live audio stream to a telephone bridge, so that participants could actually listen to the audio portion of a live online event on a telephone.

Another interesting possibility involves using an online meeting room in conjunction with a live in-person event. A library or library-related organization could offer a live event where some participants are sitting together in an auditorium while other participants are in a live online room. In essence, the live event has two live audiences. Often over the course of a live event these two live audiences meld into one.

It is even possible to offer a live event in three (or more) locations. The Alliance Library System in Illinois has had events that involved a live in-person audience, a live virtual studio audience in a Web conferencing online room, and a live group of avatars in Second Life.

INTRODUCTION TO ONLINE MEETING ROOMS

Online events typically occur in online meeting rooms,that often are provided to libraries and library-related organizations by Web conferencing services. Most Web conferences are made possible through a hosted service. In other words, everyone involved in the Web conference, including the organizers, connect to the online event using software hosted on a server managed by the Web conferencing service. This helps smooth out the bandwidth demands. For this service, you may need to download and install a small Web conferencing client program, such as Adobe Connect or GoTo

Meeting, but the real heavy duty computing that makes the online event possible is done on the host computers of the Web conferencing service.

Although this arrangement is common, it is not universal. Some large organizations, such as universities, large corporations, and large governmental agencies, may prefer to locally load the Web conferencing hosting software directly on a server that that individual organization controls.

Some Web conferencing companies do offer for libraries (singly or in groups) the option to download the hosting software and operate it on a server that the library owns and manages. Some Web conferencing software companies even offer no hosting service. They just make the software available for downloading and installing to a server operated by the library organization, which may have purchased or leased the software.

The other possible option, discussed in greater depth below, is of the virtual studio audience. These are the people who attend a live online event by entering the online room where the event is being held. The virtual studio audience usually is dispersed geographically, although small groups of people who are part of the total virtual studio audience may be in the same physical location. For example, of 100 people attending an online event, 6 of them may be in the same physical location. If those 6 people are sharing one computer connection, technically they are occupying only one "seat" in the online room.

The online room is where the online event organizers, presenters, and members of the virtual studio audience meet for the online event. The online room looks like a screen of a computer application. It may be maximized to fill the entire screen of the participant's computer monitor, resized to occupy only a portion of the participant's computer screen, or minimized while still remaining open and functional: a participant may have the online room minimized on her computer yet still be able to hear and speak with others in that online room.

An online room is often broken up into sectors which appear as different panes on the application window. For example, an embedded browser window may occupy one section of the online room, while a text chat input form and a list of text chat messages already posted to the room may occupy another part of the screen. Some Web conferencing software interfaces may include separate windows for private text chat conversations, video-over-IP images, and so forth.

Although each online room will be configured differently, according to software capabilities and user needs, here are a few general design principles and ideas. Individual users of the online room should be able to customize their experience of the room to a certain extent. The customizations should be persistent over both time and across rooms using the same Web conferencing platform. Specifically, each user should be able to resize each section of the online room to meet his or her immediate needs and preferences. For instance, if an online event involves many presentation slides and much co-browsing, but little text chatting, the user should be able to increase the relative size of the embedded browser window and decrease the size of the text chat section.

Furthermore, as the service director, you will want to be able to customize the appearance of the room so that the color scheme used by your library or library-related organization, any appropriate logos, and other organizational customization needs can be met. Usually these top-level customizations are done using an administrative module.

In addition to these customizations, there are some added features that you can use to improve the security and quality of the online room. Most online rooms have an entry screen that is basically a Web page where the visitor to the online room inputs their name, password, access code, or other information before entering the online room proper. The better entry rooms also clearly indicate to visitors where they are about to go. Furthermore, these rooms may provide information about the upcoming live online event, including the usernames of people who already have entered the same online room. The OPAL collaborative has dozens of online rooms, most of which have the same basic look. One way to help visitors know if they are in the right place in cyberspace is to clearly label both the foyer Web page and the online room itself.

Entry Web pages can provide many other types of information as well. If some sort of software plug-in will be automatically downloaded to the visitors computers when they enter the online room, the entry point could inform them of this. If there are required or recommended computing power, network connections, operating systems, and browser brands and versions, the entry point should convey this information also. Some entry Web pages allow users to test their network and audio connections before they actually enter the room and offer pop-up windows in addition to the core sectors to enable other types of functions, such as surveys, application and desktop sharing, private text-chat, and multimedia presentations.

KEY CONCEPT NUMBER 1: THE ONLINE STUDIO AUDIENCE

To understand how live online programming works, two key concepts must be understood: the notion of the online studio audience and the reality of online seats. The people who attend a live online event can be called the online studio audience. They come into the online meeting room and experience the online program as a live event. They can ask questions, make comments, and even make their own recordings of the events they attend. If they text chat, speak using voice-over-IP, or anything else during the taping of a live online event, their activities become part of the archived copy of that event.

The audience of an online event greatly influences the length, depth, and quality of the event. A fascinating phenomenon in some online programs is that occasionally in the online studio audience there are people with a greater (or at least different) knowledge of the topic than the speaker. When this happens during an in-person program, these experts in the audience have to wait for the brief Q&A session at the end. In an online session, however, these experts can share their expertise with the online studio audience during the event.

Further, the size of the online studio audience affects the energy and dynamics of the online group behavior. A group of 20 people online may behave quite differently—and require different types and levels of support —than a group of 150. The smallest online studio audience I have experienced is zero. No one other than the presenter and I (I served as the producer and technical support) attended the live online event. Some online presenters feel completely comfortable speaking to an empty or sparsely filled online room. Others may experience difficulties becoming energized and focused on the topic of their talk or presentation. As we'll discuss later, there are reasons for going ahead with an audience of zero. In contrast, the largest online studio audience I have experienced was well over 1,000. A holocaust survivor was telling her life story to multiple groups of grade school children gathered in auditoriums around the world. With a crowd that large, you can expect lots of text chatting, questions to the presenters, and tech support issues.

Holding the attention of an online studio audience can be difficult. As the presenter you have no knowledge of, or control over, each real life environment of those participating in the online event. In the real world, a participant can be distracted when someone stops by his or her cubicle. I have also heard reports of severe thunderstorms, fire alarms, and other calamities that have dragged members of an online studio audience away from the online event. Added to these random events, some software even allows members of the virtual studio audience to divide their attention during an online event. In the tcConference Web conferencing system from Talking Communities, users can minimize the entire room on their screens and work on other tasks while continuing to hear the audio portion of the online event. Even within the embedded browser window within the online room, individual attendees can browse unilaterally at will, if the online room has been configured to allow that.

Although it could be difficult to hold the attention of the online studio audience, there may be some solace in the fact that the facilitator of an online event rarely knows who is paying attention. When speaking at an in-person meeting, workshop, or event, there are few things more disconcerting to a speaker than to look out and see a significant percentage of your audience nodding off or heading for the exits. If someone exits an online event, generally everyone has knowledge of that, but snoozing is much more difficult to detect.

Ideally, participants should be able to at least know the names (or "noms de online event" because people usually can enter any name they choose) of the other participants. Even better would be to enable the participants to announce their names as they enter and communicate with each other, preferably in a way that does not intrude on the "main message" of the presentation itself.

So, who exactly are these people who attend live online events? Online programs have an amazingly broad appeal and attract a truly diverse audience. But classifying and categorizing the audience can be difficult because of the vast population that is available to attend. They vary widely across all the major seismic demographic lines, such as age, educational attainment, and income. Homeschoolers, computer buffs, the elderly, visually impaired individuals, and other groups often are well-represented at live online events. The one thing they have in common is Internet connectivity and the knowledge and willingness to attend live online events. Consider the online programs offered through OPAL. With these programs, it is not uncommon to have two or more continents represented during an online event.

A broadly distributed audience is encouraging but challenging. One of the biggest challenges to online programming is the global nature of usage. When allowed to manifest itself, the global nature of usage of library collections and services is breathtaking. The globalization of usage has far outpaced the globalization of resources and programs. For example, in OPAL, within the space of a few days we had a library user from Brazil participate in an online book discussion group, followed by a library user from Colombia who attended an online interview, followed by an information professional from New Zealand who attended an OPAL orientation session. One way to govern and control this "natural" globalization of usage of online libraries is to require users to register.

Although the online crowd is as diverse as any real crowd that gathers to attend some live in-person event, for a program manager it may be useful to develop and remember a typical or ideal user. For example, you may want to imagine your ideal user as a computer-savvy adult with broad interests but a busy schedule. By having such a person in mind, you can imagine his or her interests, experiences, and preferences.

Back in 1998 I was invited by the library director of a small community college in west central Illinois to give an evening talk about ebooks. Although Illinois overall is the sixth most populous state in the nation, west central Illinois is a sparsely populated agricultural region. I like to think this is the primary reason why my talk did not attract many in-person participants, only a half dozen or so. Nevertheless, we had a lively conversation about the excitement of electronic books and their potential to transform reading. I remember in particular one woman who attended. She lived on a farm with her husband and children, but she was not really a "farm wife," straight out of some Norman Rockwell painting. She was amazingly knowledgeable about ebooks and the ebook movement in general. Her questions and comments were thoughtful and well informed. Despite all of the national and international conferences being held about ebooks in the late 1990s, she obviously was not in a situation where she could attend and participate. This small talk at the local community college was perhaps her sole opportunity to meet with like-minded people and discuss her keen avocational interest in ebooks.

As I recall that small in-person meeting of nearly a decade ago, I have come to realize that that woman approaches the ideal person for whom live online programming would be a boon. She clearly had lots of intellectual curiosity beyond her daily activities in her particular geographic area (although I have no reason to believe that her husband, children, and "real world" friends were country bumpkins and local yokels). She was interested in ebooks and ereading, and had evidently done a lot of online research and reading about electronic books.

The popularity of an online event may be difficult to figure. However, having a live, virtual studio audience is not absolutely essential for a successful, useful online event. Consider the fact that the revenue generating capacity of a motion picture does not depend entirely on the number of people who view the film in theatres in the United States. Major motion pictures go through an elaborate series of overlapping revenue generating cycles, which may include promotional tie-ins with fast food restaurants, tee shirts, plush toys, board games, and other bric-a-brac, attendance at non-U.S. theatres (often the make or break factor for the profitability of many motion pictures), DVD rentals and sales, on-demand viewing in hotel chains and on airplanes, novelizations, and more. In a similar, but currently simpler fashion, the size of the virtual studio audience is not the sole determinant of the interest in, or popularity of, an online event. If an online event is recorded, that recording can be placed in an easily accessible archive or podcast, burned to CD and/or DVD, and manipulated in other ways to extend the reach, impact, and usability of that content.

Even if no one attends a live online event, you may want to proceed with it, primarily to get the recording that can be archived and podcast. Sometimes you may want to deliberately use a Web conferencing room as a recording studio, with no one in the online room other than the person or persons who are making the recording.

As was mentioned previously, for one OPAL event we had zero participants. We went ahead with the live online event, however, because we wanted to record the event and add it to our archive, where we were fairly confident that the recorded event would receive some use. Furthermore, as the coordinator of the OPAL online programming collaborative effort, I sometimes go into a room by myself to record a brief recording of upcoming live online events. My goal is to make a good clean recording, not to attract a live online audience.

KEY CONCEPT NUMBER 2: ONLINE SEATS

In an in-person meeting space, such as a lecture hall, meeting room, or convention center, the notion of a "seat" is fairly obvious and self-evident. Each room has so many square feet, and at any given moment it contains so many chairs. The local fire marshal may place an upper limit on the number of people who can occupy each in-person meeting room at any given time. As an in-person event organizer, I have been known to "borrow" seats from other nearby meeting rooms to meet the pressing needs for seats in my own room—without exceeding the maximum capacity specified by the fire marshal, of course. Late arriving and overflow attendees of a live, in-person event may stand in the back or along the walls, sit on the floor, or cluster just outside the room in the hallway.

In an online meeting space, "seat" has a slightly different meaning. A seat basically is the ability of one computer to connect to the server that is hosting the Web conferencing software that makes the live online event possible. If an online room has a capacity of 100 seats, this means that at any given time up to 100 computers can be connected to the Web conferencing server that brings that online room into existence. As soon as those 100 computers connect to the Web conferencing server, the room is full. After the room is full, anyone else who attempts to enter the room (that is, to establish a computer connection with that room) will be turned away. As far as I can tell, the local fire marshals of the world have nothing to fear about packed online meeting rooms.

Although a 100-seat online room has an upper limit on how many computers can be participating in an online event, the number of people actually participating in that same live online event is mushier, and subject to fluctuation and estimation. Two or more people can be "connected" to a computer that in turn is connected to the server that contains the Web conferencing software. For example, three colleagues may be in an office cubicle all looking at and listening to one computer that is connected to a live online event. Or, an entire in-person auditorium may be packed (may need to call the file marshal on that one) with an in-person crowd of people who are all viewing and listening to a live online event that is coming across one computer in the room, then being projected onto one or more large screens.

Note that it is fairly easy and accurate for Web conferencing reporting systems to monitor the number of computers connected to an online meeting room at any given time, but it may take some polling and estimations to calculate the number of individuals who actually attended a live online event. In the end, the Web conferencing system is more concerned with how many computers are connected to its server; while as the service coordinator you will be interested in how many people actually experience the live online events you plan and conduct. Seat counts may not tell the entire story. For the monthly reports I compile for the OPAL service, I try to report both the number of seats occupied during a live online event as well as the estimated number of people who experienced the live event online.

Keep in mind that if you are the coordinator of an online programming initiative, you may be made responsible for seat management. Most Web conferencing vendors lease a certain number of seats for a certain period of time, such as a day, a month, or a year. All they really care about is that you do not exceed the maximum number of simultaneous computer connections that you have leased. You can spread that seat capacity over as many rooms as you wish. For example, if you have leased 100 seats for a year, you could have a 50-seat room for larger events, five 2-seat rooms for in-depth reference interactions and other one-on-one online meetings, and two 20-seat rooms for smaller meetings.

You can even switch the capacities of your rooms to meet changing needs over the course of the subscription year. You may need to temporarily increase the size of a particular room to meet the anticipated needs of a particular online event scheduled for that room. When that event concludes, you merely return the room to its "normal" capacity. You want to have plenty of seats in the room for each online event you conduct, so that no one ever gets turned away.

In order to do this, it is possible to overload your seat capacity that is spread across several rooms. Even though your annual subscription agreement may specify that you have a maximum simultaneous seat capacity across all created rooms somewhere in the hundreds, you may be able to create a set of rooms that collectively have a seating capacity in the thousands. In general, what most Web conferencing services offer is access to a certain number of "occupied seats" (that is, computers connected to the server farm of the Web conferencing service). For example, for years OPAL had a 600 limit on the number of occupied seats we could have at any given time. We could create online rooms that collectively had many more seats than that, however, on the safe assumption that more than 600 of those, say, 3,000 seats would never be occupied at the same time. In essence, you are betting that the entire number of occupied seats across all the online rooms you have created will never exceed the maximum capacity specified in your subscription agreement with your Web conferencing vendor. This usually is a safe bet. Just as a manager of an electric company has to focus on that hottest day in July or August when energy consumption is at its peak, as the manager of an online programming initiative, you need to focus on those points in time when the largest number of the available seats may actually be in use.

If a library's Web conferencing program ever exceeds the limit, usually some sort of message is sent to the users telling them that the online room is full and they should try to connect later. Some service providers may exceed the subscriber's capacity on a particular day, if needed, on a spot basis without charge, and some services may have specific language in their contractual agreements with libraries and library-related organizations that, if the agreed upon capacity is ever exceeded, they will increase capacity on a spot basis, but charge some sort of surcharge.

Remember, if your online programming effort is continental or international in nature, time zones are your friend here. The different peak times in each time zone help spread the total use of seats over the hours of the day. So, even if 10 A.M. on a weekday proves to be a period of high demand for seats (that is, a high number of seats are occupied), that 10 A.M. hour arrives at different moments in universal time. As a result, the demand on the server farm actually is spread over a half day or so (and thus tends to smooth out the high demand over time).

WHAT IS THE PURPOSE OF ONLINE LIBRARY PROGRAMMING?

Two essential questions regarding online public programming are, Why should a library do this, and how can a library do this well (where "well" includes the basic concepts of efficient, effective, and sustainable programming)?

The purpose of an online library programming initiative is to produce and distribute online programs that help the participating library pursue its mission of providing information and information services to its user population. The goal is not necessarily to replace in-library and other in-person programs, but rather to provide another venue for public events and continuing education programs that prove to be informative, convenient, and enjoyable to the participants. If Web conferencing software enables a library or library-related organization to efficiently and effectively achieve its public programming goals, its goals for organizational communication, and its goals for staff development, then there is no reason not to use the software.

One way for your library to do online programming well is to collaborate with other libraries to start a service. The usual advantages of collaborating —the ability to share start-up and learning costs, the ability to spread the financial risk, and the ability to quickly achieve a critical mass of good programming and expertise—apply in this situation, too.

CONCEPTUAL CONTEXTS FOR ONLINE LIBRARY PROGRAMMING

Be wary of assuming without much reflection that online programming is nothing more than taking the in-person live programs that libraries have been organizing and presenting for decades and delivering them online. As more library programs are delivered primarily or exclusively online, new forms of programs may emerge. All successful online programming must capitalize and exploit (in the good sense) the affordances—that is, the qualities of a system or environment that encourage individuals and groups to engage in certain actions with and uses of the system or environment (see http://en.wikipedia.org/wiki/Affordances)—of the Web conferencing medium being used.

One affordance of Web conferencing is the disassociation of auditory and visual communication. While a person is speaking, others may be conveying information via text chat or via co-browsing on the Web. When these three simultaneous channels of communication complement each other, as the group communicates overall, the resulting depth, complexity, and richness of communication can be inspiring. Often, however, one mode may diminish another mode of communication or just introduce noise. The chat communication can distract everyone—both the speaker and the audience members—from the primary auditory message.

Live and interactive are the two touchstones of online programming. In the fall of 2005 a state library association made most of the sessions at its annual conference available for viewing and listening to anyone online. These streaming audio and video Web broadcasts were impressive. They were well produced and well directed. As I watched and listened, however, I quickly experienced an intense desire to interact with the speakers and others experiencing these conference sessions, both the in-person and online attendees. Unfortunately, there was no way to do that. There was no text chat option. The audio and video were a one-way broadcast, with no opportunity to ask questions. I couldn't even tell how many other people were experiencing these conference sessions online. I had no idea how large the virtual studio audience was.

It was, in short, an experience very similar to watching television. The broadcast model that dominates television is not a good model for wide emulation by live online programming. The possibilities for speaker-audience interaction, and even audience-audience interaction, are just too vast with Web conferencing to ignore or underutilize. Web conferencing is a great way to foster and facilitate online social networking. Adopting a broadcast mentality will not suffice, nor will it survive in the online era.

Although live online programming generates a certain energy and natural human attractiveness that prerecorded programs cannot, there are many instances where prerecording portions of what will be predominantly a live online event makes sense. For example, if a speaker wants to explain a complex process or idea in efficient, effective terms, a well-rehearsed and prerecorded segment may be in order.

There are numerous aspects of in-person events that are difficult or impossible to replicate online. Nonverbal communication is much more difficult to conduct online compared to in person. Some text chat components of Web conferencing systems may offer emoticons, but it is not the same as seeing a person actually smile or frown.

Although online programs do not involve people congregating in one geographic location, an online sense of a group gathering can be fostered and conveyed to the participants. At the very least, people like to have a sense of how many other people are attending an online program. One good thing about online attendance figures in an online environment, compared to attendance numbers at an in-person event, is that at an online event the attendance need not be portrayed in comparison to the size of the room. At an in-person conference, a presentation attended by 50 people in a room designed to hold 50 seems like a packed, popular event. However, if the same number of people attends the same event in a room designed to hold 500, it may appear to be a lethargic, poorly attended in-person event. This is the bane of the existence of many an in-person conference planners. He or she has to determine beforehand how many people are likely to attend each conference event so that each room is neither too big nor too small for the number of people who actually attend. Because in many Web conferencing software systems the total capacity is not displayed to the attendees, those 50 attendees are never placed in the context of the size of the room.

Live programs also add some intangible benefits. The value of *live* online public programs needs to be explicated and perhaps even defended in this era of highly polished, mixed, prerecorded, synthesized media presentations. In the end, it all boils down to the human warmth factor. In their early days, the Internet and the Web often were experienced by many as cold, lonely environments. You could FTP files, go to highly structured Gopher sites, and even participate in some text-based multi-user dungeons and other rudimentary online environments, but it all seemed impersonal and distant.

Email brought some epistolary warmth to the online environment, but the warmest letter only goes so far. A picture may paint a thousand words, but reading a thousand words to get the picture sometimes can be tedious. Text chat increased the sense of human warmth in that the user was actually conversing with someone (whether it was a human, a dog, or a droid—an intelligent robot—always was a nagging point of suspicion, however). Voice-over-IP increased the warmth factor, bringing some immediacy and nonverbal communication (namely, voice inflection, pace, pauses, and nonverbal utterances) to the online environment.

Other media, such as radio and television, seem to be moving away from live programming. Sporting events are one of the last bastions of live TV and radio. And if the sporting event you are watching has half time with some sort of live entertainment, you can rest assured, thanks to Janet Jackson, that you will not be watching it absolutely live on your TV.

Live online programming, warts and all, has a certain basic human appeal similar to live television and live radio. *Saturday Night Live* sounds much more interesting and attractive than "Saturday Night Prerecorded."

Nevertheless, the value of recording, archiving, and podcasting online programs should not be underestimated. Basically an online programming initiative should strive to find and use as many distribution channels that make sense for the clientele and are within the library's means (in terms of time, money, and technical expertise).

Certain media, such as newspapers, television, and radio, are predominantly broadcast media. They focus on one-way communication, from one to many. The letters to the editor section of a newspaper and call-in talk radio shows are two notable exceptions to the general rule. Nevertheless, I think we can safely say that these media are essentially—both historically and in terms of underlying technological infrastructure—broadcast media.

Live in-person programs can be either primarily the broadcast or interactive variety. A lecture basically is a broadcast (one to many) typically followed by a question-and-answer discussion, while a good book discussion is much more interactive and participatory.

There are many new ways for librarians to reach out to their user population, such as blogs, vlogs (video blogs), podcasts, and screencasts (a video recording of your computer screen, often with voiceover supplied by the computer user, that is then broadcast). Online programs—both for the general public and for librarians and other information professionals—can serve as a major piece of the puzzle of this emerging system for communicating, creating compelling content, and organizing digital information. Online programming is evolutionary, not revolutionary. To understand the importance of this evolutionary change, it may be useful to compare it with what happened to the library catalog in the last half of the twentieth century. Around 1970 the library catalog underwent yet another format conversion. The card catalog was converted to an online catalog. This required a lot of retrospective conversion of bibliographic information. Card catalog cabinets were replaced by computer terminals. In most transition instances, the reality of dial access to the online catalog arrived some time after the switchover from the card catalog.

Online programming also involves a format change. Rather than traveling to a real space where a live in-person program is held, attendees use their Internet-connected computers to enter an online room where the live online program is held. Compared to the library catalog migration, there is little need for retrospective conversion. Perhaps some wordprocessed documents and presentation slides would need to be converted to HTML and uploaded to a server, but that is about it.

Another interesting difference between the great library catalog conversion and the transition to live online programming is that remote access is integral to the notion of live online programming. Although it does occasionally happen that people come to the physical library to attend a live online program, that is not the primary venue for accessing these programs.

Finally, although in quite a few instances once a library had converted from a card catalog to the online catalog, the card catalog was also kept around (and sometimes updated) for awhile; this was mainly for risk management and political reasons. In the long run, it is expensive and unnecessarily redundant for a library to maintain two catalogs. Obviously, the online catalog ultimately replaced the card catalog. The same may not happen with live online library programming. There is no reason to believe that ultimately live online programming will completely replace live in-person programming. Each mode has its strengths and affordances.

OBSTACLES TO A SUCCESSFUL ONLINE PROGRAM

Before you can launch a successful series of online public programs, you must address and overcome two basic obstacles. The first is to impress upon potential attendees that online programming is not a complex technology for end-users with a long learning curve. Keep in mind that librarians can be as reticent about participating in live online events as end-users. Our experience has been, however, that most people become acclimated to the online meeting environment in less than 15 minutes. Although the idea of online programming may be difficult to describe and understand conceptually, it is easy to learn through experience.

The second big obstacle is an impression that some librarians form—that designing, creating, producing, and delivering online public programs is more complex and labor-intensive than doing the same for a traditional in-person public program. This generally is not true. Preparing for an online presentation may involve some different planning strategies (e.g., be sure to test your microphone beforehand!) and a slightly different set of skills, but the complexity and labor involved in preparing for an online event is not appreciably greater than preparing for a in-person event.

CONCLUSION

Library Programs Online really is a long argument—admittedly very early in the life of online programming initiatives offered by libraries—for the value and potential of this type of effort. I am generally enthusiastic about, and see the opportunities in, online library programming. Throughout the book, however, I try to place online programming into context, taking a long hard look at its limitations and realistic trajectory of development.

The advantages of online conferencing for a wide variety of library-supported events—public programs, staff training, and professional development—cannot be ignored. Bell and Shank (2006) make a succinct, compelling case for online conferencing when they said, "That's the beauty of virtual conferencing. It saves time and money, provides expanding opportunities for professional development from any computer connected to the

Internet, and allows you to access archived content. It eliminates worries about creating backloads of work while you take time to travel for learning." Web conferencing also is more environmentally friendly than most in-person events, especially if attending these events require a significant amount of travel.

2

Online Programs and Online
Programming Services in Action

CHAPTER SUMMARY

Because you may be unfamiliar with or only vaguely understand the concept
and reality of online library programming, in this chapter we explore some
examples of existing and emerging online library programming efforts. We'll
also take a look at some similar but distinct movements, such as online
distance education programs at graduate schools of library and information
science.

INTRODUCTION

Organizing this discussion around existing types of face-to-face public
programs (such as interviews, demonstrations, lectures, seminars, concerts,
gallery exhibits, debates, and more) may help you make sense of what is possible in Web conferencing environments, how these events relate to your
existing program formats, and how they differ. Each type of program has
its own dynamic, and its own set of nuances.

The development of live online programs in Web conferencing environments is somewhat reminiscent of the early years of television. It may have
taken television broadcasters a few years to figure out that, although a 60-
minute variety show (based on the old vaudeville live shows), the 30-minute

sitcom, and the 60-minute drama show all are part of television, they each have their own forms, dynamics, and core set of viewers. Here we examine some of the options in terms of online programming and discuss ramifications regarding forms, dynamics, and audience. The chapter concludes with some patterns and generalizations across all types of programs.

TYPES OF ONLINE PROGRAMS

Interviews

Interviews are relatively easy to produce and they are engaging and popular. The natural human interaction between the interviewer and interviewee has a certain innate appeal to most people. Conducting a live interview online does not diminish any of that natural appeal. If your library or consortium is planning a series of online interviews, there should be a defining theme to help connect the individual interviews and build a recurring base clientele.

For example, OPAL has initiated an ongoing series of monthly "casual conversations" with leaders in librarianship. The program format is casual, with impromptu forays into non-library-related subjects (food, fun, and so on). Laughter is encouraged. They are held on Friday afternoons and last no more than one hour. Prior to each casual conversation I jot down some potential topics and questions the interviewee and I may want to discuss, but there definitely is no scripting. This type of interview format seems to work very well in a Web conferencing online room.

In the fall of 2008 the American Library Association, under the leadership of ALA President Jim Rettig, began a series of interviews and discussions called the Connections Salon. The basic idea is to encourage librarians to come into a Web conferencing online room, listen to an interview with a special guest on a topic, then engage in informal, informed, and free-flowing conversation, reminiscent of the Parisian salon culture of yore. The Connections Salons take the basic idea of an online interview, combine it with a salon atmosphere, give each session a little thematic structure, and encourage all librarians to participate.

Online interviews in general work wonderfully. Usually approximately 20 questions can be asked and answered in one hour. The interviewer should prepare at least 25 questions beforehand to share with the interviewee prior to the presentation so that the interviewee has a sense of what will be asked. If you are interviewing someone with something to sell, such as an author with a newly published book, an artist with a collection of work, or a vendor representative, you may want to gently remind them that people will attend the online event to learn primarily about the person and the projects and products in which she or he is involved, not to hear an overt sales pitch.

If you are the event organizer, meet with the interviewee (as well as with the interviewer, if appropriate) prior to the online event to make sure the interviewee's microphone is working and that the he or she feels comfortable and confident in the room. If your online programming initiative does not have a formal permissions procedure, during this informal pre-event online meeting with the interviewee, you may wish to ask the him or her for permission to record the online interview, archive it on the Web, and podcast the audio portion of the recording. If the interviewee grants permission, and they almost always do, you will not have a paper trail of the granting of permission, but you personally will know that the interviewee has been informed of your intent to record, archive, and podcast, and that he or she orally consented.

If you offer online interviews, be sure to leave plenty of time for a question-and-answer period with the members of your virtual studio audience. Because text chatting is a ubiquitous feature of Web conferencing systems, members of the virtual studio audience may ask questions—and comment in response to what the interviewee is saying—throughout the interview. If you are organizing and facilitating the interview, inform both the interviewer and interviewee beforehand, and the members of the virtual studio audience at the beginning, that questions can be posted at any time, but they will be addressed during the Q&A period. As the event facilitator, you may want to perform some triage on the questions, such as grouping by topic and roughly ranking them, during the interview so that the interviewer can quickly spot the more interesting questions that have come in during the interview. If private text chatting is available with the Web conferencing service you are using, you can use private text chat to communicate with the interviewee about which questions he or she may want to address.

Because interviewees often are leaders in exciting fields, some controversies may have accumulated around their activities. This may result in hecklers attending your live online interview event as members of the virtual studio audience. If this happens, the good news is that they cannot throw pies, rotten fruit, chairs (a la Geraldo), or other projectiles at the interviewee. But, they can verbally heckle the interviewee and disrupt the interview through text chatting and voice-over-IP comments. As the manager of an online programming service, you should anticipate this type of development and explore how the Web conferencing system you will be using can help with crowd control and thwarting hecklers.

Also, be prepared with policies and procedures for handling hecklers, even if those policies and procedures are not fully articulated. For example, you could begin your response to a heckler by using private text chat—text chat between only you and the heckler—to warn the heckler that his or her language is unacceptable. Be sure to identify yourself as a representative of the online programming service that is sponsoring this online event. If one or two private text chat messages do not dissuade the heckler, you can warn the heckler that he or she will be ejected from the online event if the behavior doesn't stop. Many Web conferencing systems will allow you to eject an individual from a room. If the heckler pops back in and continues heckling, it may be possible to ban the IP address that the heckler is using from ever entering that room again—or until you lift the ban. Another option is to eject the heckler again, then lock the room. However, keep in mind that if you lock the room, no one can enter until the room is unlocked. Late-arriving non-heckling members of the virtual studio audience will be excluded, too.

Although in five years of providing online public programming using Web conferencing software I have never witnessed a serious case of heckling, the possibility always exists. When we were planning for a program about the life of a Holocaust survivor, the planning group had a serious discussion about how to respond if someone who denies that the Holocaust ever occurred should attend and confront the presenter in a hostile or belittling manner. We decided that, if the heckler was simply denying the Holocaust, we would not eject him from the online room. But, if the heckler became verbally abusive to the presenter or to other audience members, we would begin a process starting with private text chat warnings to the heckler about the abusive language, which, if unheeded, may have led to ejection from the online room.

Lectures

The lecture format also works well in online meeting rooms, assuming the lecturer feels comfortable with the technology and is able to convey a sense of warmth. Because most Web conferencing software offers voice-over-IP, pushing Web pages (co-browsing), and presenting PowerPoint slides, a lecturer usually has as many communication tools available—if not more—than in the typical in-person lecture event.

Be sure to invite the lecturer into the online lecture room prior to the start of the event, not only to test his or her audio connection, but also to get the lecturer acclimated as to how the online room operates as a lecture space. The goal is to have the lecturer feel comfortable about the technology and the communication mode so that he or she can concentrate on the topic of the lecture, not on the technology.

Try to set up a time to meet online with the lecturer a day or two before the online lecture, rather than an hour or two before the start. That way, if there are technological problems, you will have plenty of time to resolve them. However, having the lecturer arrive in the online room at least 15 minutes prior to the start of the online event is also a good precautionary measure, in case the lecturer has developed some audio input or output problems at the last minute. Knowing that the lecturer has arrived will ease your mind as the program planner, too! Also, because many lecturers travel, and because Web conferencing online rooms are accessible from just about anywhere with an Internet connection, be sure to test the connection, if possible, from the geophysical location from which the lecturer will actually be presenting. We have had lecturers present from hotel lobbies, college residence halls, homes, and other non-work locations, usually with great success.

One specific question to ask the lecturer concerns how to handle text chatting during the lecture. Often a lecturer can lose his or her train of thought or become flummoxed by reading the text chat while speaking. Many lecturers may prefer to have someone else monitor the text chat and report back with major points raised and questions asked. In some Web conferencing systems, each participant can modify the look and feel of the interface to meet his or her needs and preferences. The lecturer, for instance, may want to minimize or hide the text chat message area to reduce the risk of distractions coming from the Web conferencing interface itself.

One potential downside to any one-hour lecture—online or in person—is that one person basically does all the talking. To hold a group's attention for an hour when nonverbal communication is minimal is a difficult fete to accomplish. During online lectures, participants lack the nonverbal clues and interesting distractions that make listening to a lecture sustainable. Participants cannot even observe the other members of the online virtual studio audience, although in some Web conferencing systems two or more participants can engage in private text chat. Many providers of Web conferencing systems have provided some live video capabilities, but because many users of webcams often situate their cameras so that only their heads are visible, and because of the poor quality of many video transmissions over the Internet, the introduction of live video to Web conferencing is not going to improve significantly the ability to communicate nonverbally (for example, via hand gestures) using this medium.

Because many (but not all) lecturers want to present some slides or engage in co-browsing, be sure to work with your lecturer so that their slides are ready to present in the Web conferencing online room. If you know beforehand that the set of presentation slides are going to be made available in the online archive area of your programming effort, it makes sense to load the slides in the archive and present them from there. That way, you don't need to move them after the conclusion of the online event. If the URLs of where the lecturer wishes to co-browse are available before the lecture, you may want to put them in the archive as well, and have someone copy and paste each URL into the text chat at the appropriate point during the lecture so that members of the virtual studio audience have access to the URLs via text chat, too. The Library of Congress often does this during their monthly online programs.

If you are planning a "combo event" where the lecturer will be presenting to both an in-person and online audience, orient the lecturer in advance as to how that is going to work. Briefly explain, for example, how the audio systems works for both the in-person and online crowds. For instance, if your lecturer tends to move around quite a bit while lecturing, work with the lecturer and the sound technician (which may be you!) to make sure that the lecturer's audio is picked up by the microphone leading into the online room. The Henry Morrison Flagler Museum in Florida has considerable experience with organizing and delivering these combo events.

Orientation Sessions

The goal of many online programs is to introduce and orient the participants to a specific collection or body of knowledge. Often this involves both teaching and delighting the audience. Libraries, museums, archives, and library-related organizations with special collections and outstanding or unique cultural riches may find this type of online programming particularly useful as a way to introduce a target service population or the general public to the library's collections.

The Library of Congress has created and delivered a series of monthly online programs through the OPAL collaborative that basically provide brief, focused glimpses into the wealth of their massive and diverse collections They have programs focused on sheet music from the Civil War era, birdseye view maps, early motion pictures, chocolate, and other topics. The Lincoln Presidential Museum and Library also has presented "Lincoln Rarities"—realia from their collections—in an online program that was very well received. These programs attract a diverse virtual studio audience, from scholars to homeschooled students. Of course, orientation sessions also can be presented about the Web conferencing software itself.

Training Sessions

Training sessions tend to work better if the online group is smaller—less than a dozen participants. Participants feel more comfortable in a smaller group, and they will feel they have better access to the instructor.

Training sessions may require more functionality than other types of online events. During training sessions there may be a strong need for whiteboarding capabilities, where the screen functions like a whiteboard that can be scribbled on, where the trainer can see and control what's happening on each trainee's desktop, where password-protected Web sites can be demonstrated and explored in depth, and so on. In many online training sessions it is imperative that participants see the trainer's cursor, see form fields as they are being filled in, and more.

07), the Blended Librarian Online Learning Community "offers
ebinars on topics related to its mission. These are open to all
nd membership in the community is free." In 2008 the Blended
offered live online events on participatory librarianship, the user
, intergenerational service challenges, breakthrough instructional
s, and more.

versity (www.clickuniversity.com)

niversity offers a diverse suite of e-learning opportunities, with a
son courses sprinkled into the mix, to library and information sci-
ssionals who are members of SLA, the Special Libraries Associa-
w.sla.org). Some of the learning opportunities are live
ous), while others are "replays" from a previously recorded ses-
casts, or self-paced learning modules. SLA awards IACET
nal Association for Continuing Education and Training) CEUs
ng education units) for some of the courses and programs offered
Click University. Most of the e-learning opportunities offered
Click University are available only to SLA members.
f their self-paced courses have been clustered into Professional
ent Libraries. For example, they offer over 60 courses in the Lead-
d Management track, over 70 courses in the Organizational and
Improvement track, and so on. Six-month and one-year subscrip-
hese clusters of self-paced courses are available. Individual courses
ed a la carte, with pricing beginning at $8 per course.
University offers a live online series of programs—Click U Live!—
zes the WebEx Web conferencing system. It appears that these live
ograms last approximately 90 minutes, and pricing is based on each
connection, not on the number of people attending at any particu-
on. For example, if five people attend a Click U Live! program in a
ce room, they would pay for only one connection or seat. One sam-
online program held in December 2007 was a 75-minute presenta-
Gary Price about searching using search engines. The price per
eat was $15. A 90-minute live online seminar on Project Profiles cost
seat.
University also records many of their live online events and offers
the archive through their Replay service. The cost for members to
Replay recorded online seminar is $69. Podcasts of sessions at pre-
A in-person conferences for which the speakers and facilitators have
permission to record and podcast are available at no charge to SLA
s through the Click University service.

Book Discussions

Book discussions are a natural for the online event environment. They are
mainly about dialogue, so voice-over-IP, bolstered by text chatting and co-
browsing, works well. The key to a successful online book discussion series
is to develop a core group of participants who generally participate on a
regular basis—month after month, if it is a monthly book discussion. An
ongoing book discussion can be of a general nature, including both works
of fiction and nonfiction, current books and older works, including classics.
Or it can focus only on fiction, perhaps even on a particular genre, such as
mysteries, romances, science fiction, or historical fiction.

One problem with book discussions of any sort is that attendees are
expected to have read the book prior to the discussion. This tends to keep
the group small. If people have not "done their homework" by finishing
the book, they may be reluctant to attend, even if only to lurk. It has been
my experience, however, that often it is the people who have not yet read
the book, or have not yet finished it, who seem to be most engaged in and
energized by an online book discussion. At the conclusion of such discussions, these "lurkers" often express their fervent desire to read or finish the
book that was discussed.

However, for some reason, online book discussions do not draw as well as
one would imagine. Often book discussion attendance in OPAL is in the single digits. With online book discussions, there is no opportunity to meet with
others face-to-face, and participants need to supply their own refreshments.

One technique to increase attendance at an online book discussion is to
extend invitations to author centers for an author being discussed. For an online discussion of *My Antonia* (1918), Willa Cather's novel, we invited faculty
members and graduate students from the Cather Project at the University of
Nebraska at Lincoln to participate. Many did, and it was one of the better online book discussions I have ever experienced. The recording of that book discussion received lots of usage out of the OPAL Archive, as well.

The online event environment can be used for an enhanced book discussion where images of the author or of places or things pertinent to the book
can be co-browsed. Virtual worlds take this notion a step further by creating
virtual environments that mimic real and fictional places, such as the Globe
Theater, Victorian London, and Green Town from Ray Bradbury's novel,
Dandelion Wine (1957). Bradburyville in Second Life even contains a
"walk-in" version of *Fahrenheit 451* (1953), whereby avatars can walk into
and experience some of the key scenes and characters of that novel.

Genre Discussions

Compared to online discussions of specific books, genre discussions tend
to have a broader appeal and higher attendance rates. People who develop

a fondness for a particular genre or sub-genre often attend these online genre discussions to connect with fellow lovers of the genre, advance their claims for good authors in the genre, and to learn about other authors in the genre whose books they may want to read and explore.

Genre discussions are also popular as a professional development tool. Recently, for instance, over 20 reader advisors from libraries for the blind and physically handicapped attended an online presentation and discussion about recent fiction and nonfiction political books. These monthly genre discussions are sponsored by the Illinois Talking Book Centers, and the programs are designed primarily for the reader advisors who help blind and low-vision readers select the audio books that meet their needs, interests, and tastes in fiction and nonfiction.

Author Discussions and Literary Readings

Author interviews and readings work well in the online environment, too. Readers love to hear directly from authors, and most authors like to hear directly from their readers.

During online book discussions, genre discussions, and author interviews, it is also possible to offer a virtual book signing session. Here is how it would work: During the discussion or interview, members of the virtual studio audience are made aware of the availability of an online book signing webform. The discussion facilitator would then co-browse the entire group to the webform, or a link to the webform could be made available for individuals to pursue unilaterally. Be sure to include a field where readers can request a special inscription ("To my dear nephew ... "). The author will appreciate it if you limit the size of that field. No money or credit card information need be collected online. The completed webforms are written to a database, which can be reviewed by the event organizer or online programming service director. You will need to work with a local bookstore or the publisher of the author's book or some other supplier to make sure that a sufficient number of printed books are available at the author's location for him or her to sign. After the conclusion of the online event, the fulfillment vendor (such as a local bookstore, the publisher, or an etailer) contacts the members of the virtual studio audience who requested signed copies to confirm the order and to gather payment information. Once that step has been completed, at the convenience of the author, he or she can sit down and sign the hard copies of the books to be shipped to those who requested them.

Story Hours

As of this writing, I have not personally participated in an online story hour, nor have I heard of libraries performing this function; but it seems to

me that online story hours for childre
could read the story at the same time
book or co-browses to pertinent Web
the librarian reads the story, or, as ma
you could disable the text chatting fun
to avoid a tempting distraction.

Other Examples

One of the more innovative combo e
combined live and online battle of the
the Johnson County Library in Kansas
by the Institute of Museum and Librar
Award. The event was primarily an in-
most of the attendees were in the same
broadcast live, as an OPAL online event.
agreed to have their music recorded, arc
recordings were placed in the archive, w
ple could vote for their favorite band. In
live in-person competition also is the lea
recordings of these bands quickly becam
loaded audio recordings from the archive

ONLINE LIBRARY PROGRAMMING

Many online programming services rela
technology, and related fields have croppe
representative online programming servic
alphabetical order. This is not an exhaus
made to ensure that the information is acc

AMIGOS

The Continuing Education program of
quartered in Dallas offers dozens of online
related topics. They are using Saba Web
www.amigos.org/?q=node/536.

Blended Librarian Online Learning Com
blendedlibrarian.org)

According to the Blended Librarian Web s
blender are instructional design, technology, a

Farkas (20
periodic w
members,
Librarian
experience
experience

Click Uni

Click U
few in-per
ence prof
tion (ww
(synchron
sion, po
(Internati
(Continui
through
through
Some
Improve
ership an
Professio
tions to
can be us
Click
that utili
online p
compute
lar locat
conferer
ple live
tion by
virtual s
$99 per
Click
access t
access a
vious SI
granted
membe

EASI (http://easi.cc)

EASI (Equal Access to Software and Information) is led by Dr. Norman Coombs. According to EASI announcements, it has "provided online short, month-long, teacher-led courses on creating accessible information technology for more than a decade and has reached over 5,000 people from more than 3 dozen countries. Anyone taking 5 courses will earn the Certificate in Accessible Information Technology provided jointly by EASI and the University of Southern Maine." Some EASI online events are offered free of charge, and some involve a registration fee.

EASI also offers annual membership subscriptions for both individuals ($300) and institutions ($900). EASI programs generally are recorded and archived.

EASI uses the tcConference software from Talking Communities. The entry way into an EASI online room (http://easi.cc/entrance.htm) offers succinct but thorough information for new users. It explains which computer operating systems the Web conferencing system they use will support. It also explains what software is needed to access the room and how a small software plug-in will be automatically installed the first time a person enters an EASI online room. In addition, the welcome page explains how to manually install the plug-in, in case the automatic installation process fails. They even explain how to resolve problems with local firewalls.

Education Institute (www.accessola.com)

The Education Institute, an initiative of The Partnership of the Provincial and Territorial Library Associations of Canada, is a virtual professional learning institute that offers live audio and Web conferencing-based programs for the North American community of library professionals. The Ontario Library Association provides some organizational support for The Partnership. In 2006 the Education Institute offered over 150 online programs.

Beginning in the spring of 2007, the Education Institute's online programs expanded into the United States under the direction of the publisher Neal-Schuman. A registration fee is charged for these live online events.

The Education Institute uses the Audability Web conferencing system, which requires a telephone conference call to achieve voice communication.

Five Weeks to a Social Library (www.sociallibraries.com/course)

According to the FWSL Web site, "Five Weeks to a Social Library is the first free, grassroots, completely online course devoted to teaching librarians about social software and how to use it in their libraries. It was developed to provide a free, comprehensive, and social online learning opportunity for librarians who do not otherwise have access to conferences or continuing education and who would benefit greatly from learning about social software."

The first iteration of the FWSL online course occurred between February 12 and March 17, 2007, using the OPAL platform, which is powered by tcConference Web conferencing software from Talking Communities. The programs were recorded and archived and are available free-of-charge through the OPAL Archive (www.opal-online.org/Archive.html).

In late October 2007, Meredith Farkas, one of the organizers of FWSL, indicated that no reiteration of the online course has been planned yet, but other organizations, both within and beyond librarianship, are using the basic FWSL structure and content to meet their own online learning needs.

LearningTimes (www.learningtimes.com)

LearningTimes is a privately held corporation that offers and fosters a wide range of online and in-world workshops, events, conferences, and ongoing learning communities. LearningTimes uses a variety of Web conferencing software, including Adobe Connect and Elluminate Live.

Library Learning (www.librarylearning.org)

The Library Learning initiative launched in February 2006. They appear to be focused primarily on professional development and continuing education opportunities for librarians and library staff members. Library Learning is funded in part by the grant from the Institute of Museum and Library Services (IMLS).

OPAL (Online Programs for All) (www.opal-online.org)

OPAL is a loose federation or collaborative of libraries of all types. As of mid-2008 there were 45 organizational members on three continents: North America, Europe, and Australia. OPAL has partnered primarily with the Web conferencing service, Talking Communities, using their tcConference platform. During its brief history, OPAL also has used Web conferencing services from iVocalize and Elluminate.

A group of talking book centers in Illinois, led by the Mid-Illinois Talking Book Center, began testing a live online programming service in 2003 by providing online book discussions and interviews primarily for print-impaired users of talking book centers and libraries for the blind and physically handicapped. They quickly expanded the scope of their mission to offer online public programs for library users worldwide. After two years of testing and experimentation, the OPAL online programming collaborative officially launched on August 1, 2005. In August 2007, the Alliance Library

System in Illinois, which had managed OPAL from its inception, transferred the leadership in this collaborative initiative to TAP Information Services.

SirsiDynix Institute Webinar Series (www.sirsidynixinstitute.com)

According to its Web site, "The SirsiDynix Institute is an ongoing forum for professional development in the library community. By providing free access to industry-leading speakers and events, our mission is to support librarianship and advance the work of librarians around the world."

The SirsiDynix Institute uses Microsoft Office Live Meeting as their Web conferencing service. The public face of their programming efforts consists of large online events with major thinkers and speakers from librarianship and related fields. They also provide access to an archive of previously recorded programs and podcast the audio recordings of the webinar series.

URLearning Series from *Library Journal*

In November 2005, *Library Journal* launched its URLearning series of webcasts. The first online event was a panel discussion of recent developments and trends regarding ebooks in academic and research libraries. *LJ* secured some corporate sponsors for this event. They did not charge a registration fee, but they did ask interested individuals to register for the online event. Approximately 550 people registered for the event, and approximately 350 actually attended.

Library Journal used the company Globix to actually produce this online event. *LJ* is a division of Reed Business, and other divisions of Reed Business were already using Globix to conduct other webinars and online events.

With 350 participants focusing their attention on a hot topic, lots of comments and questions came in during the 45-minute roundtable discussion. One interesting feature of the Globix platform is the ability to conduct polls from within the online event itself, then show everyone the results of the poll. The Globix system also allows for the easy incorporation of prerecorded segments, such as messages from the corporate sponsors, into the webcast. One downside to the Globix system is that members of the virtual studio audience cannot readily discern how many people are attending the webcast. Nor can two or more members of the virtual studio audience text chat with each other. Because of the audience size and the nature of the system used, this was more of a broadcast event than a communal gathering.

WebJunction Wimba Classroom (Formerly Live Space) (http://webjunction.org/do/Navigation?category=14519)

In January 2007, WebJunction announced the launch of a new Web conferencing service for libraries, called Live Space. WebJunction partnered with Horizon Wimba, a company that offers Web conferencing software, to offer this service. The name of the service has since been changed to Web-Junction Wimba Classroom. In addition to offering a Web conferencing service to libraries, WebJunction also offers online programs of interest to librarians and library staff members.

CONCLUSION

As we have seen in this chapter, there are many types of programs for library staff members and the general public that work well in an online environment, and many organizations are offering a wide variety of live on-line events using Web conferencing software. As people continue to experiment with this medium, and as travel budgets shrink, the popularity of live online programs delivered via Web conferencing software probably will increase.

3

Developing an Online Public
Programming Service

CHAPTER SUMMARY

This chapter contains an examination of principles and tips for developing
an online library programming effort. Methods for inferring and assessing
the needs of potential users of an online library programming effort are
described. Different formats for online programs (such as an interview, open
discussion, single-person lecture, and panel discussions) are reviewed.

INTRODUCTION

An online presentation can be as much of a team effort as you want and
need it to be, or it can be a one-person show. The various components of a
successful online event can be divided up among multiple people. Components include recording the online event, providing tech support from within
the online room itself (especially audio output and input problems), monitoring the questions and comments that come in via text chat, manning the helm
of the co-browsing feature, advancing the presentation slides, and so on.

THE DYNAMICS OF LIVE ONLINE PUBLIC EVENTS

Live online events that use Web conferencing software have a slightly different dynamic than in-person events, telephone conference calls, live events

in three-dimensional virtual world environments (also known as in-world events, to distinguish them from online Web-based events), and other types of group gatherings. In one sense, they are more fragile than in-person and in-world gatherings because group members are not receiving many visual clues from other group members. Dead audio time can be very disconcerting and disruptive to a group using Web or telephone conferencing. Often prior to the official start of a live online event, the conference organizers and the presenters may be using voice-over-IP sporadically. When there is a prolonged period of no audio, simply because no one needs to test their microphones, someone who has arrived early as a member of the online studio audience will ask via text chat why no sound is coming across. As every radio listener knows, dead air time is very disconcerting.

A highly polished and professional presentation or event is not necessarily better in the Web conferencing environment. Highly polished presentations and lectures may actually serve as a mild disincentive to attendance and attention. People comprising a virtual studio audience seem to respond better to online events that are informal, unpolished, and participatory. These are commonly sought characteristics of in-world group events held in virtual worlds, too. Some presenters who are excellent as "sages on stages" during in-person presentations have a hard time relaxing and lightening up when they present online or in-world.

The Web in general is becoming increasingly participatory. When it comes to live online programs held in Web conferencing systems, one cardinal rule is keep your audience engaged. The simplest and best way to do this is to let them see who else is in the room. Because this is possible in a live in-person event, it always has puzzled me why some online event organizers withhold this simple privilege and natural human source of curiosity from their live online audiences. Another key form of engagement is to let them text chat, both "publicly" (meaning, to everyone else in the online room) and privately amongst themselves. If the Web conferencing system you are using allows private text chat between two or more people in the online meeting room, enable that feature for your online event. Trying to create a virtual sensory deprivation tank for your virtual studio audience is the absolute worst way to try to gain and hold their attention. When people attend a live online event, many of them multitask. They will check their email, browse the Web, or work on some other aspect of their professional lives while they listen. As an organizer and presenter of a live online event, you have to accept the fact that multitasking will occur, and that you cannot control or eradicate it. Most online audiences will not be giving you their full, undivided attention, and you never really can be certain how many members of the virtual online audience are multitasking. Of course, less than 100 percent attention is common in in-person audiences, too, particularly in recent years. They may be checking their Blackberries, Twittering with others near and far, or even nodding off.

ASSESSING USER NEEDS

It is difficult to assess user needs and preferences for an online programming service prior to the launch of the actual service, especially if most of the people in the target population are not already using Web conferencing for other purposes. Live online events are one of those things for which people have a difficult time gauging their level of interest and participation prior to actually experiencing a few live online events.

Once your online programming service is launched, however, you can use feedback from current online events to better understand user needs and preferences. Remember, too, to examine usage of your recorded and archived online events as another measure of demand for certain types of programs and topics.

During the early years of the OPAL collaborative we had a speaker present a series of online programs about the various tips and techniques of amateur photography. The live online attendance figures were not outstanding, but, over the years, the archive of the recorded online events has received a considerable amount of use.

The OPAL collaborative has realized that for most types of online events, one hour is about the maximum amount of time that people want to spend online exploring any given topic. If a potential online speaker insists that he or she needs more than an hour to make a presentation on a topic, consider having a break during the online event, so that people can get up, stretch, go to the rest room, and grab something to eat or drink. For long presentations that last three or more hours, you may want to consider having three one-hour sessions spread over the course of a day (say, at 10:00 A.M., 1:00 P.M., and 3:00 P.M.) or spread over three days of a week.

FINDING AND ACCLIMATING PRESENTERS
AND FACILITATORS

Every live online event requires some sort of presenter or facilitator. Even the monthly online salon events sponsored by the American Library Association, which draw their inspiration from eighteenth-century Parisian salon culture, where small groups of people gathered to discuss the hot topics of the day in an informal, relaxed setting, need some sort of facilitator or host.

The presenters need to feel comfortable with the technology so that they can concentrate on the presentation of their content and the human interaction that online programming facilitates. As mentioned previously, it is wise to meet with the presenter in an online room prior to the day of the online event so that you can test the presenter's connection, voice-over-IP, video-over-IP (if available), and so forth. You can also provide the presenters with a basic orientation to the online meeting room and how the online event will proceed. Confirm with them that it is permissible to record, archive, and podcast their presentation, and affirm with them how many components of the online event they want to manage themselves. Do they want to advance their own slides? Do they want to respond to text chat comments and questions without prompting? Do they even want to be able to see the text chatting of participants while they are speaking? Remember, if some situation arises (e.g., an audio problem or a heckler) that requires some private text chatting between the presenter and the event organizers, you will want to make sure the presenter knows how to use private text chat. Another option is to use a completely different "back channel" that is separate from the Web conferencing service you are using to communicate privately with the presenters. Instant messaging and even texting on cell phones can serve this purpose.

Even the participants of an upcoming online event may desire and need some pre-event acclimation sessions. At least during these initial years of the relatively broad acceptance and use of Web conferencing systems, many participants in your online events may be communicating using voice-over-IP for the first time. Prior to the actual online event, you could offer some times when you will be in the online room to help people test their audio input—via an embedded microphone, external microphone, headset, or other means—and their audio output—via internal speakers, external speakers, earbuds, or headphones. The control and fine-tuning of audio input and output may require quite a bit of tweaking by each individual participant, both within the Web conferencing software itself and in the control panels of each participant and presenter. During online events it is not uncommon for some participants to report that the speaker is too soft, while others report that the speaker is too loud. (There always are a few Goldilocks for whom the speaker is just right.) Some Web conferencing software may allow you to raise or lower the volume of individual speakers.

FREQUENCY OF ONLINE PROGRAMS

Another aspect of overall program planning and strategy to consider involves determining the frequency and regularity of individual programs within the overall online programming initiative. Some online programming initiatives go for the "big cannon" effect, booming out a big program that draws hundreds of attendees every month, or even every quarter. The Sirsi-Dynix Institute's webinar series and Library Journal's URLearning series seem to fit this pattern. Another strategy is to provide more online programs with greater frequency, but with smaller attendance at individual events; examples include EASI and OPAL (Online Programs for All). Rather than a big cannon booming out large online programs periodically, initiatives such as OPAL are more like BB guns, persistently peppering cyberspace with online programming opportunities. Some programs may draws hundreds of people to the live online event, while others will draw fewer than ten.

The advantage of the big gun strategy is that the organizing team for these infrequent events does not become exhausted and the potential virtual audience for your programs does not develop online event confusion and fatigue. Realistically, the only way an online programming initiative can follow the BB gun strategy is if it is a collaborative effort involving several libraries. The advantage of the BB gun strategy is that you are able to offer more— and thus a wider variety—of online programs. With proper planning this enables your initiative to offer something for everyone.

EXPERIMENTING WITH DIFFERENT PROGRAM FORMATS

Basic Building Blocks of an Online Event

The basic building blocks of online programming include

- text chatting,
- voice-over-IP,
- co-browsing,
- presentation slides,
- polling,
- testing,
- video-over-IP,
- prerecorded content,
- display or collaborate in real time on other applications, such as word processors and spreadsheets,
- whiteboard activities, such as highlighting and underlining, and
- recording.

Interactivity is Crucial

Interactivity is often one of the most appreciated aspects of an online program. Review with the presenter what modes of supported interactivity work well with the type of online presentation being planned, as well as the communication style and comfort level of the presenter. Some presenters prefer to hold questions until after the conclusion of a formal presentation. Other presenters welcome and seem to draw energy from interesting questions or comments expressed at any time during a presentation. In most online meeting rooms, however, there are more options available than the just the hold/don't hold option that in-person presenters face. In an online meeting room attendees can be encouraged to type in questions and comments as they come to mind during a presentation. The presenter may announce at the beginning of a program, however, that he or she will read and address the comments and questions only during natural breaks in the presentation or at the end. Some presenters find it difficult to continue speaking cogently as they read incoming text chat comments and questions.

Including Prerecorded Segments

Software programs such as Camtasia and tcScreen can be used to pre-record segments of a live broadcast. These can include segments that would be difficult to convey well in a live setting, or that involve a level of detail and complexity that may require multiple "takes" to get right.

Initially it may seem counterintuitive, but an essential component of many successful live online programs is often the prerecorded segments. Consider your nightly television newscast, where live and prerecorded segments are interwoven into a seamlessly whole program that is conveyed and experienced as a live broadcast. That's how it works in online programming as well.

Not Too Long, Not Too Short

Any type of communication medium or live event tends to develop a sense of an optimal length. Most motion pictures last between 90 and 120 minutes —shorter for children's movies. The 50-minute college lecture has become the stuff of legends. The ideal length for the typical live online event appears to be about one hour. Because people are busy, and because many participants may be at work when they are attending a live online program, in your announcements of upcoming events you should include an estimate of the duration of each.

TIPS ON THE SUCCESSFUL MANAGEMENT OF AN ONLINE PUBLIC EVENT

The essential elements of a successful online event are few in number: a good, easy to learn, easy to use, and reliable Web conferencing service; a lively, relaxed, and informed speaker on an interesting topic; and an alert and interested virtual studio audience. Of course, the other efforts and contributions to an online event are not superfluous, and they can add significantly to the overall quality and success of the online event. If, however, as the program director you concentrate on these three essential elements, in nearly every instance you will deliver a successful online event.

Danger, Will Robinson: It is possible to overproduce an online event. If an online event contains too many prerecorded segments or is too scripted, your virtual studio audience may develop a sense that the online event is canned or phony. There is a delicate balance between having a live online event that is too unscripted and too unfocused, versus one that is too scripted, polished, and rehearsed—and sometimes even prerecorded. My experience has taught me that most people—at least people interested in information technology topics—do not like to hang out online and just have a free-flowing conversation. They like a presentation or at least some structure to the conversation. There should be some sense of a moderator or facilitator. Nor does the audience want to watch a canned program.

Another argument against over-engineering an online event is that it can lead to rapid burnout on the part of the event organizers. By agonizing over every detail and contingency of an online event, the organizers often are reluctant to replicate it ad infinitum. Although most online events are one-shot deals, to have a successful online programming initiative you need to weave together an ongoing string of successful one-shot events.

Another thing to consider is what attendees experience prior to the start of an online event. What are they seeing and what are they hearing? Sometimes background music can be provided prior to the official start of an event. Other times the event organizer and the presenter are performing some last minute checks of the system. Often the early arriving attendees are engaged in text chatting or conversing using voice-over-IP.

There is one fundamental problem with delivering global online programming that may be very difficult to overcome: there are more than 24 time zones around the world. When it is early afternoon on Tuesday in Missouri, it is evening in Europe and very early Wednesday morning in New Zealand. No time chosen for an online program can meet well the diurnal rhythms of library users worldwide.

The pacing of an online event may need to be slightly different than for a live in-person event. The tolerable length of dead audio time is much shorter for a live online event than for a live in-person event. One potential reason for this low tolerance for quiet think-time during an online event is that some people may begin to wonder if they are experiencing audio difficulties.

One crucial point in most live online events where the dead audio time issue comes to the fore is when the speaker or presenter pauses to let members of the virtual studio audience raise questions or make comments. He or she needs to give people a chance to articulate their questions or ideas, but the presenter must also be mindful of the overall low tolerance level of most virtual studio audiences for dead audio time. To keep the pace moving, consider utilizing the chat function of your program. If everyone attending the live online event can see who else is in the online room, and if there is some visual indication when one or more attendees are typing, this typing signal will indicate to everyone that a question or comment is forthcoming and will ward off the dead air time anxiety that quickly builds.

Remember, even if a live online event that your initiative sponsors and delivers contains some dead audio time, the recording software associated with Web conferencing programs will often automatically delete periods in the recording session when no audio or video activity occurs. Thus the recordings of most online events that last approximately one hour when experienced live often are only 45 to 55 minutes in length when experienced as a recorded online event.

COSTS, BUDGETS, FUNDING, COST RECOVERY

The largest expense of starting and maintaining an online programming service is human labor. It takes time, expertise, and talent to develop and promote the overall program, as well as the individual online events. Depending on how large the program is you are starting, it may take as much as one-quarter of a full-time position to devote to this service.

Some of the work can be done by volunteer in-kind efforts from participating library units or member organizations in a collaborative program, but ultimately, someone needs to be in charge of the overall program and all facets of the program.

The second largest expense will be for the Web conferencing service. Libraries and library groups can spend about as much or as little as they want on an online programming service. If you have never window shopped for Web conferencing software, prepare for sticker shock. Much of this software was developed for large corporations and the U.S. Department of Defense, so it is priced accordingly. Some Web conferencing vendors are beginning to realize that the potential market for this software extends to smaller companies, smaller governmental agencies, and not-for-profit organizations such as libraries. Even free, open-source Web conferencing systems are available now. Following is a list of Web conferencing systems, both free and fee-based, that are known to be used by libraries and library-related organizations:

- Adobe Connect (http://tryit.adobe.com/us/connectpro/webconference/?sdid=DJZGI)
- DimDim (www.dimdim.com)
- Elluminate (www.elluminate.com)
- GoToMeeting from Citrix (www2.gotomeeting.com)
- Microsoft Live Meeting (http://office.microsoft.com/en-us/livemeeting/default.aspx)
- Saba Centra (www.saba.com/products/centra)
- tcConference from Talking Communities (http://talkingcommunities.com/solutions_tcconference.html)
- WebEx (http://webex.com)
- WebHuddle (www.webhuddle.com)
- WebTrain (www.webtrain.com)
- Wimba from Horizon (www.wimba.com)

The actual yearly expense will depend on which vendor (or vendors) you use for the program, the number of seats you require, and other variables. The most inexpensive cost per seat per month I have encountered for what I consider a viable and adequate Web conferencing hosted service is $1 per seat per month. The most expensive is over $20 per seat per month.

If your library or collaborative organization does not already have access to some server space for the Web site and the associated archive of recorded online programs, you will also need to have a hosted Web site service. Good hosted Web sites can be leased for under $25 per month. If you want to purchase a Web site template to jumpstart the development of the Web site for your online programming service, good templates can be purchased for less than $50.

Assuming that your library or library-related organization already has an adequate supply of Internet-connected computers, the only equipment expense may be for computer microphones and/or headsets. Many desktop computers come with an inexpensive microphone included in the box. Ask the IT staff at your library or organization if they have any spare microphones. They may have a drawer full of them. Most laptop computers have built-in microphones. The inexpensive computer microphones, available at discount stores such as Wal-Mart and Best Buy for less than $10, seem to work fine.

Is it possible and advisable to sell advertising "space" at live online events? Of course. Sponsors for the entire public online programming effort can be sought, as well as sponsors for individual speakers, events, workshops, and conferences. It also is possible to offer online space for exhibitors at online conferences.

GOVERNANCE

If an online programming service is initiated by a single library, in most instances the governance of the service will fall under the existing governance structure for the library as a whole. If, however, the online programming service involves more than one library or library-related organization, the options and challenges for governance of the service multiply.

One way to govern an online programming service is to have a governing board. For example, in an online programming collaborative each member organization could appoint one person to the governing board. If two or more libraries or library organizations share an organizational membership, they can appoint only one person to the governing board. Advisory committees and working groups can also help with the governance, growth, and refinement of an online programming service.

One basic question you should answer is whether the service should become some sort of legal entity, such as a not-for-profit corporation. That way the program itself can handle money, seek outside funding, be sued, and other fun stuff. Each online programming service and their parent organization, if any, will need to make that decision.

STAFFING

One of the challenges of staffing a live online programming initiative is that such an initiative, while small in the overall library mission, requires a wide variety of skills and competencies that usually are delivered in small but timely doses. Pre-production, production, and post-production skills, Web site creation and maintenance skills, promotional skills, and communication skills all are needed. If only one person is going to serve on the "staff" of your online programming initiative, you need to find a "compleat renaissance" person, or at least someone willing to learn these various competencies on the job. If you decide to divide and conquer this menu of widely varying tasks, no single individual needs to devote much time to building and sustaining the initiative. The danger with following this route, however, is that it may take much longer to pull all the pieces together. Personally, I think the jack-of-all-trades route is the better path of the two to follow. One danger with following this route, however, is that other staff members in your library as well as users of the service may come to closely associate the program with that person. Some of my colleagues call me "Mr. OPAL." The initiative may be perceived by some as that individual's pet project. If that person eventually takes another position within or outside of your library, it may be a significant blow to the identity and momentum of the initiative.

MANAGEMENT

The day-to-day management of an online program involves developing program ideas; maintaining and tending the Web site and the calendar; recording and archiving recordings of programs; podcasting the audio portions of recorded programs; providing training and orientation sessions for staff at member organizations, presenters, and the general public; organizing and facilitating meetings of any boards, working groups, advisory groups, and user groups; announcing and promoting upcoming programs; and more. Managing an online program demands continuous attention and a wide variety of skills. Because a large part of managing an online program involves preparing for, facilitating, and wrapping up live online events, for OPAL online programs we have created a sequential checklist for moderators (www.opal-online.org/moderatorchecklist.htm) to review and execute at each stage of the production process.

WEB SITES AND PORTALS SUPPORTING ONLINE PROGRAMMING SERVICES

Before people can participate in online events, they usually visit a Web site to view the schedule of upcoming events, learn the technical requirements for participating, and access the archive of recorded programs.

In addition to a Web conferencing system, a library-based online programming service also needs a Web site to serve as the focal point for the service. The Web site serves as a vehicle for announcing upcoming programs, provides links into online events, supplies technical information and help, collocates information about the service and the organizational members (if the service is a collaborative project), organizes the archive, and gathers feedback from users of the service. This support system does not absolutely, positively need to be a Web site. A wiki or podcast could serve the purpose, too.

One basic purpose of the online programming service Web site is to announce, structure, and provide entry to upcoming online events. An online calendar is one good way to handle these tasks. An embedded shared calendaring system for these hosted Web conferencing systems is beneficial to a collaborative public programming service in that it allows the developers of online programs at the member libraries to input their events on the Web-based calendar.

On the online programming Web site you will want to provide overview and background information about your online programming service. Be sure to include press releases, system and service enhancements, announcements of new organizational members, and other current information.

Another key function of the service Web site is to provide access to archived programs. These are live online programs that have already occurred but have been recorded in some way. For example, only the audio portion or perhaps the audio, video, text chatting, and co-browsing of the live online event may have been recorded. From an archive you can also provide links to the separate components of an online event, such as any documents or "handouts" that were displayed during the online event, the presentation slides, a related blog, or a wiki.

Visitors to the service Web site will expect an overview of available technical support. Provide troubleshooting guides, FAQs, and contact information for technical support. If troubleshooting is a triage effort involving the service management team and the Web conferencing hosting service, make sure this portion of the service Web site clearly indicates how the triage process works.

If the online programming service you initiate or are involved in is a collaborative service, be sure the Web site prominently displays the list of organizational members. Include information on the Web site about how organizations can join the collaborative or consortium.

The Web site for an online programming service requires constant care and feeding. New content is being added to the Web site, the archive, and related areas on a daily basis. Older content needs to be updated or removed. As the coordinator of this initiative, you will want to make sure that you or your designee is tending the Web site on an ongoing basis.

TECHNICAL SUPPORT

Providing technical and troubleshooting support over the Internet from a distance can be difficult and frustrating both for the tech support person and the person seeking assistance. One rather delicate challenge in many technical support situations is to suggest that operator error may be a contributing cause to the situation without alienating or offending the person you are trying to assist. Often, when broaching this topic, I mention sad but true tales of my own stupidity and ineptness, such as the time I had my PC microphone plugged into the headphone slot (Why didn't they design those two slots originally to have different diameters?), or the time I had not pushed the microphone cord completely into the slot in the computer, or the time I had muted the entire audio output on my computer.

Providing technical support and troubleshooting services before and during live online events can be challenging. Before the event begins, attendees should be encouraged to enter the online meeting space or test their overall computing environment (meaning, operating system, RAM, bandwidth, versions of necessary software) to make sure that they can get connected and participate.

Computer microphones, whether embedded or external, prove to be particularly troublesome. It is essential that any speakers, presenters, or facilitators of an online event test their connectivity and the basic features of interaction and communication to make sure that everything is working properly. The good news here is that getting presenters and attendees acclimated to an online meeting environment is almost always quick and painless.

One very effective way to minimize the number of technical and procedural questions during a live online event is to allow attendees to test the connection, their equipment, and their knowledge of how the online room works prior to the actual start of the live online event. Some live online programming initiatives offer a text link or room that enables potential attendees to an upcoming online event to test their connection and computer configuration and to become at least minimally aware of how the online room is configured and works.

QUALITY ASSURANCE

Quality control is difficult to ensure down to the level of the single online event. Sometimes a speaker who was great in person at a conference you attended six months ago will, for whatever combination of reasons, be a dud online now. Some presenters simply cannot become comfortable with the online Web conferencing environment. Sometimes they report back to me that they had no idea how much they rely on nonverbal feedback from the audience until they didn't have access to that information in the Web conferencing environment.

There are, however, several techniques you can use to maximize the quality of online events. First, make sure that your presenter has a basic knowledge of how the online meeting software works and that he or she is reasonably comfortable with it. This usually entails testing the online event environment with the presenter before the actual event. This also is a good time to test the presenter's microphone and audio connection.

Another technique is to have the presenter focus on the topic and the human-to-human interaction, rather than on the technology. Someone else can be the designated person to advance the slides, deal with technical questions and glitches, and so forth.

Last, because most online event systems offer two or more channels of communication, such as voice-over-IP and text-chatting, the richness of the communication can be distracting to a presenter. It can be difficult to follow text chat when one is speaking. It may be worthwhile to have someone else be the designated person to monitor the text chat, and then interject into the voice-over-IP communication salient points and questions from the text chat stream. An added bonus to this "divide and conquer" strategy to a successful online event is that the audio recording of the event also will contain the best information that came through on the text chatting channel.

SECURITY ISSUES

Just as libraries, conference halls, convention centers and other bricks-and-mortar public meeting locations have security issues, online public meeting rooms have their own unique set of security issues.

Most Web conferencing software allows rooms to be open all the time. This allows for people interested in attending an upcoming event to enter the room, become acclimated, test their connections, etc. The downside is that "virtual squatters" may begin using the online room for their own meetings, happenings, or trysts. The usage reports for each online room will reveal this activity after the fact, but how can a manager of an online programming service prevent this type of unauthorized use of an online room?

For the types of online programs that libraries and library-related organizations typically offer, crowd control, jeering, and online hecklers have not been a major problem to date. Everyone seems to be remarkably civil and well behaved. The type of virtual studio audiences that online library programs attract tends to be a little different than the type of audiences that attend tapings of television game shows or *The Jerry Springer Show*. An added plus. in online environments there are no opportunities for fisticuffs or the flinging of chairs.

Some online programming initiatives make their online meeting room accessible only from a half hour before the start of an event until a half hour after the conclusion. The EASI service, for example, offers a test room that is capable of holding only one person. This allows a newbie to test his or her connection and learn how these online rooms work while limiting the options and chances for abuse and misuse of the online room.

Other initiatives leave their online rooms open all the time. The advantages of having rooms always open is that it is easier for the program coordinator and the management team to coordinate the rooms, and interested individuals always can pop into the room to look around, test their connection, and get a direct experiential sense if attending an online program would help meet their information needs, their need for more and better professional development opportunities, and/or their need for a sense of belonging to a community.

CONCLUSION

Developing, managing, and sustaining an online program service for your library or library-related organization is not rocket science, but it does require a wide variety of skills, patience, and persistence. Whether you are the sole staff person of the service or part of a team, you will want to develop routines and lists of best practices and quick fixes to problems that may arise.

$$\underline{\hspace{9cm}} 4$$

Web Conferencing Systems

CHAPTER SUMMARY

Now that networked computers are widespread in libraries, homes, and offices, Web conferencing software is the key piece of technology that makes online programming services possible. This chapter summarizes the software used to create and deliver online library programming. The roots of Web conferencing software are explored, followed by an analysis of features, usability, accessibility, and reliability, especially for voice-over-IP and other high-bandwidth-demand features. This chapter also explores the administrative modules that support online events, as well as the types of usage reports available. Finally, you will find information about other software programs that can support an online programming effort.

INTRODUCTION

Some hardware and software devices perform rather straightforward activities. A flatbed scanner, for instance, creates scanned images. Of course, there are many ways to tweak the production and output of those scanned images, but scanning is the main and self-evident function of that flatbed scanner. The same holds for a barcode reader. Although it can be calibrated in different ways, its primary purpose is to read barcodes.

Other hardware and software devices are more like a tabula rasa that can be developed into a sumptuous smorgasbord. This type of hardware and software is more inchoate and enabling than the more single-purpose type of technology. Given a sufficient number of Lego blocks, time, and imagination, just about anything could be built.

Web conferencing software is a "tabula rasa" type of technology. Individuals and organizations can use it for a wide variety of purposes. Libraries and library-related organizations can use Web conferencing software for intraorganizational meetings, interorganizational meetings, conferences, workshops, training sessions, forums, advanced online reference service, and public events.

Web conferencing software enables groups to hold live online conversations, meetings, programs, conferences and other events from distributed geographic locations. It can serve as an adequate substitute for in-person conversations, meetings, programs, and conferences, and it beats the telephone hands down because it offers more communication channels (voice, text chatting) and is much cheaper, assuming that individuals and organizations already have made a long-term commitment to networked computers and are looking for new, effective ways to leverage their investment.

Online library programming services use Web conferencing systems developed for other types of organizations and sectors of society, such as large for-profit corporations, educational institutions, and branches of the military. I would argue that libraries have a rich tradition of "riding on the coattails" of technology originally developed for other purposes. We can and do learn from how other types of organizations and services exploit these technologies. Just as call center software has expanded its purpose to encompass virtual reference services, so too can software developed originally for online business meetings and online formal learning experiences (e.g., higher education courses for credit) be re-purposed to meet the needs of online library programming.

Web conferencing software is similar to other types of software that may be used by libraries and library users. Online forums and message boards, instant messaging services, virtual reference software, and webcasting software are examples of software with functionality and design that may be similar to Web conferencing software. The Web Conferencing Guide developed by "think of it" (http://thinkofit.com/webconf/index.htm) contains useful background information and links about the entire field of software and services that make real-time conversations, meetings, and events possible over the Internet.

Most but not all Web conferencing services require all participants to download and install a small software plug-in. Some services rely entirely on Java to make their service work, thus avoiding the need for a separate plug-in. WebHuddle and ReadyTalk are two examples of plug-in-free Web conferencing services that run in most browser software without special plug-ins.

Web conferencing software qualifies as the forgotten tool of the Library 2.0 movement. In all of the recent hullabaloo about the Web 2.0, social networking systems, and Library 2.0, people have championed blogs, wikis, plogs (a blog devoted to a particular project, such as a new building project for a library), and other cool tools, while overlooking the fact that the best way to build communities and social networks is to converse. For a long time, the primary limitation on the power of conversation was the fact that all of the conversants had to be within earshot of each other. After mail allowed people to communicate in writing, and the telegraph enabled coded communication over distances, the telephone came along and enabled conversations over vast distances. More recently, a wide variety of synchronous and asynchronous methods for conversing over a distance have been developed, including email, instant messaging, and using voice-over-IP and text chatting via Web conferencing software. Selecting a Web conferencing platform is little like selecting an integrated library system, although on a smaller scale. All of the vendors appear to offer the same core functionalities, but there are key differences in price, accessibility, reliability, the proprietary nature of the software and its components, and other factors.

The problem with most Web conferencing systems is that they seem to have been developed primarily for Fortune 500 companies and the U.S. Department of Defense. Hence they tend to be feature rich and prohibitively expensive for most libraries, library consortia, library associations, and related organizations.

Instant messaging software and internet telephony software, such as Skype, are getting to the point where they also could be considered as a basis for delivering live online programming. Many of these software programs now offer VoIP and video capabilities via webcams. One potential limitation of these classes of software is that, at least currently, there are often rather severe limits on the number of people who can participate in any one online event. They may be adequate for small group discussions and small online training sessions, but not for larger three-digit gatherings. Another potential limitation is in most instances of software that fall in either of these groups, the ability to quickly and easily record an online event for later distribution and use is either nonexistent or very rudimentary.

LIBRARY-RELATED USES OF WEB CONFERENCING SYSTEMS

Libraries and library-related organizations can and are using Web conferencing software and systems to achieve a wide variety of organizational goals that rely on real-time communication. Some of these uses are outlined below.

Fully Public Events

These are events that are open and available to anyone worldwide with access to the requisite hardware, software, and connectivity. When libraries offer online events to anyone in the world, it often is amazing how geographically dispersed the attendees are.

Semi-Public Events

These events may be open only to a defined subset of the population. For example, a public library may announce and promote an online event only to its geographically defined primary clientele.

Private Meetings and "Conference Calls"

Web conferencing software can be used as a substitute for, or improvement upon, the traditional telephone conference call. Often people can speak either in half-duplex ("walkie-talkie") or in full-duplex modes.

Online Reference Room for Advanced, In-Depth Reference Interactions

Some libraries and library consortia are using Web conferencing software for advanced online reference services. The librarian on duty may be in the room, waiting for a patron to enter. When that happens, often there is some sort of visual and/or audible clue to alert the librarian that service is required. To maintain the confidentiality of the reference interaction, the online room may become full (and thus closed to intruders) once the online reference patron arrives. Many Web conferencing systems may be configured so that recording the session is very difficult or virtually impossible.

Recording Studio

Although the focus of this book is on live, real-time online events, please note that Web conferencing software can be used as a recording studio. The person or work team making the recording enters the online room, turns on the recording feature, goes through as many "takes" as needed, and then works with the resulting recording(s) to make a polished recording available to library staff members or the general public. A fuller examination of the recording studio is made in Chapter 8.

Virtual Office

Some librarians have been known to use an online room supported by Web conferencing software to hold online office hours.

Loanable Room for Authorized Non-Library Groups

Some libraries treat their online rooms—made possible by a Web conferencing system—the same way they do the physical public rooms they manage. Recognized groups in the community, the campus, or the organization may reserve and use the Web conferencing room.

CRITERIA FOR SELECTING A PLATFORM

What we have discovered is that different types of online events require different types of functionality. Some online events require whiteboard capabilities and sharing desktop applications, while others do not.

Be mindful that imagining the use of Web conferencing software by your library or library-related organization may be quite different and more complex than the actual use your organization will make of a Web conferencing system. The bells and whistles of a system may dance in your head like sugarplums in the dreams of children during the holiday gift-giving season. Be realistic and practical during this visioning process. Just as the bells and whistles of online catalogs sold them to deans, directors, and search committees, but are rarely used by actual users of the system, some of the bells and whistles of Web conferencing systems sound great, but raise the price, make overall implement and use more difficult, and receive little actual use.

As you evaluate, compare, and contrast various Web conferencing systems, develop a decision matrix portraying the various functionalities, costs, hardware and software requirements, tech support, and various intangible factors that are important to your library or library-related organization. Score or weight each decision variable both in terms of the need for your online programming service and the quality of that function offered by each Web conferencing vendor. The use of spreadsheet software (see http:// en.wikipedia.org/wiki/List_of_spreadsheet_software for a list of various types of spreadsheet software) can make this task more manageable and flexible.

One interesting aspect of online programming via Web conferencing systems is that it exists both as a form of human communication and as a network for the creation and distribution of content in the form of digital objects, including Web sites, databases, audio files, presentation slides, and the like. In considering possible criteria that could be used to select a platform for your online programming service, you may find it useful to differentiate between the service as a communication medium and as an engine for the creation of, distribution of, and interaction with content. The content may take one or more forms, such as Web pages, presentation slides, doodling on a whiteboard, word processing documents, spreadsheets, and image files. If you plan to use Web conferencing software primarily for online events that are heavy on group-based communication, such as panel discussions, seminars, and meetings, you may want to focus on the communication features of Web conferencing software. If, on the other hand, you think most of your use of Web conferencing software will be used by single presenters of lectures, workshops, and other types of online events where one person basically is speaking and presenting content, you may want to focus more on the features of Web conferencing software that enable to effective presentation of a wide variety of content (such as slides, documents, password-protected Web sites, and media files).

Operating Systems Supported

As of September 2008, Net Applications, Inc., (http://marketshare .hitslink.com/report.aspx?qprid=8) estimated that 90 percent of all personal computers were running some version of Microsoft Windows (Vista, XP, 2000, 98, etc.), 8 percent some version of the Apple Macintosh operating system, nearly 1 percent were running Linux, and the remaining 1 percent spread across a wide variety of other operating systems. Mac OS and Linux users, however, tend to be more tech savvy, affluent, and vocal than the average bear.

For Web conferencing companies that use a client software program to deliver their online meeting experience to users, this market share pie for computer operating systems presents a challenge. By developing a client software that works on computers running the fine Microsoft family of operating systems, they can reach 90 percent of their entire potential market. But they feel compelled to develop flavors of their client software that will work on computers running the Mac or Linux operating systems, because these users are often opinion leaders.

Communication Channels

Web conferencing software in general provides a rich palette of real-time communication options, with an attractive cost-benefit ratio. Let's briefly examine some of the main communication channels usually available via Web conferencing.

Text Chat.—Text chatting is a common way of communicating during a live online program. Participants in the live online event type alphanumeric characters to form words and sentences to send comments, questions, and ideas to all other participants in the live online event. Private text chat communication within a public online program is also an essential component to success, especially in an instance where the presenter need to communicate with someone who is providing tech support.

Often text chatting involves copying and pasting text chat from other applications into the text chat window within the online room you are using, so make sure this works with the Web conferencing system you have selected. During an online event it is not uncommon for participants to serve as "Baker Street Irregulars" (an allusion to the street urchins that Sherlock Holmes used for various purposes) for the main presenter, who go out and find URLs, Wikipedia definitions, and other tidbits that support the flow of the presentation and discussion. Text chatting can be one-to-all, one-to-one, or one-to-a-few. Of these three forms of text chatting, the third (in essence, a small group conversation within a larger group attending the live online event) seems to be the most infrequently encountered functionality, so you may want to look specifically for that, if it is an important functionality for your organization. Most Web conferencing services offer one-to-all and one-to-one chat.

Voice-over-IP.—If text chatting is the cake of communication within an online room, VoIP is the frosting. Voice-over-Internet Protocol is the means for delivering voice (and, generally, sound) communication over the Internet and other packet-switched networks, thus obviating the need for a separate telephone conference call. At the very least, the software system selected for a live online programming initiative should enable the presenter to speak to the virtual studio audience. Ideally, any members of the virtual studio audience who have microphones connected to, or embedded in, their computers should be able to speak as well.

By 2008 the use of voice-over-IP for online programming was fairly widely diffused, accepted, and used. There still were a few Web conferencing systems out there that were using traditional telephony to carry audio information, but they were becoming rare birds.

Much has been written about social networking on the Internet and the emerging "read-write" culture, where people feel empowered to comment on and "talk back" to what they experience online. Of course, it's possible to talk back to your TV, newspaper, and other forms of broadcast communication, but no one hears you, other than your family members, your pets, and, if you are really riled, your neighbors. The text chatting and VoIP communication options within most Web conferencing services encourage this form of "read-write" and "hear-talk" participatory social networking. This can be a little disconcerting to presenters at online events who expect a more traditional "read-only" relationship with the participants in the live online event. They want to be the sole speaker (until opening up the Q&A session), and they expect the participants to "listen-only" and "read-only." VoIP and text chatting, however, when used in the context of live online events conducted using Web conferencing software, have a tendency to diminish the differences between the presenter and the audience. Imagine an in-person conference program in which everyone has equal access to a microphone. No one needs to sidle down a row of chairs to approach a microphone in the central aisle. Everyone can speak and text chat while sitting comfortably in chairs.

Nonverbal Communication.—One of the knocks against Web conferencing communication as we know it is that it tends to be weighted far too much in favor of verbal communication. Spoken words transported via voice-over-IP and written words communicated via text chat often dominate a Web conferencing event. Nonverbal communication can include facial expressions, hand gestures, and other body language. It even can include the clothing one is wearing and the ambient environment in which one is living while participating in an online event. Some Web conferencing systems have tried to incorporate nonverbal communication into the mix with limited success. Elluminate, for example, offers its Web conferencing participants the ability to smile, frown, look confused, raise one's hand, and clap. The current version of tcConference from Talking Communities offers so many emoticons that it can be difficult selecting just the right emoticon to express your current emotion that you wish to convey to the group. Am I just angry, or really angry with a red face?

While nonverbal communication can be an important component (some theorists argue that it is the most important component) of human-to-human communication, remember that these attempts to incorporate nonverbal communication into the mix of live online events are a bit artificial. It is one thing to see an actual smiling face, and quite another to see an emoticon of a smiling face. Seeing a flapping hand on screen is not the same as hearing applause in person, neither for the speaker nor for the audience.

Video-over-IP.—The big development on the horizon at the time of this writing is the wide-scale adoption and diffusion of video-over-IP. Video-over-IP allows a video image, such as that produced by a webcam connected to your computer, to be sent and received over the Internet using the Internet Protocol. The addition of streaming video to voice and text chat represents a big change, and also a greater demand for bandwidth.

The value of video-over-IP for an online programming service remains open to healthy debate. Some see video over IP as the final piece of the online programming puzzle that will put it on a par with in-person programming. Personally, I remain skeptical that streaming video will add much to the online programming experience. It even could have a negative effect on live online programming because it will be perceived as talking heads. Many people may want to see the visage of the speaker, especially just prior to and during the opening moments of a talk, when a few obligatory jokes often are tossed out like candy at a parade, but once the presentation begins, many people just want to focus on the information and the ideas being conveyed.

Online Polling and Testing.—Many Web conferencing systems offer the functionality to conduct online polling and testing. The polling can be premeditated and carefully planned or spontaneous on the part of the presenter and/or organizer of the live online event. (One can only hope that all online testing is premeditated and carefully planned.)

Even if the Web conferencing system your library is using does not have an online polling function, you always can use the text chat functionality to perform some free-form polling. For example, at the start of live online events it is not uncommon for the presenter to ask the participants to type in their institutional affiliations and geographic locations. Of course, this method of free-form polling via the text chatting feature cannot provide easy tabulation of results on the fly. All you can do is quickly eyeball the results to get a general sense of how people have responded to your impromptu poll.

In many Web conferencing systems, however, it is possible to save text chat as a file (usually a simple text file that can be pulled into any text editor or word processing program) for later detailed review and analysis. For the OPAL online event sponsored by the Bensenville Public Library in Illinois on September 11, 2006, where a Holocaust survivor spoke, the organizer of the event, Bill Erbes, did a great job of getting the word out about this free online event to school districts around the nation. Many school districts arranged assemblies centered around the event.

During this live online event we could tell how many computers were connected to the room, but we could not tell how many people were attending at each location. So we conducted an impromptu poll using text chat. We asked people: If there is more than one person at your physical location listening to this holocaust survivor speak, please type into text chat the number of people at your location. There were 158 computers connected to the online room at that time, so the text chatted numbers came at us fast and furious. I saved the text chat for that live online event and went back and put all the attendance numbers reported into a spreadsheet. The result: over 3,500 individuals—mainly school children—listened to that holocaust survivor speak through those 158 computer connections.

The interesting thing about online polling is that you can capitalize on the ease and immediacy with which information and feedback can be gathered —and captured—in an online environment. During a live *in-person* event it is easy and immediate to provide feedback, too—through clapping and shouts of affirmation or contradiction, for example—but unless the conference organizers have an applause meter set up and ready to use, it is difficult to document and capture the nature and amplitude of this type of immediate feedback during a live in-person event.

In reality, the online polling I have experienced while attending live online events merely functions to affirm what the speaker and/or organizer already suspected about the audience's response to what is being presented. I do not recall a single instance where the speaker seemed to be truly surprised by the results of an online poll.

Show Me the Content

As mentioned above, communication and content are the two work horses of any live online event. Another essential component of any online library programming initiative is being able to access the various types of content needed for a successful program. The content needed may include other Web sites, proprietary databases, information from other applications (such as documents and spreadsheets), other media files (images, audio and video clips), presentation slides, and canned components. The challenge with content is to be able to easily and effectively pull content into an online meeting room so that participants can see it—and perhaps interact with it in different ways.

Co-Browsing

Synchronized browsing, or co-browsing, is one essential way to share content in an online room. This feature allows the speaker or presenter to take the online audience to a specific sequence of Web sites and Web pages. The person in control of the co-browsing feature has control over what is being presented to each live online participant. Typically, the presenter or his or her designee turns on the feature of the Web conferencing software that forces the embedded browser in the online room to present to every participant wherever on the Web the presenter goes.

Co-browsing generally works well when the person in control of co-browsing is taking everyone to public portions of the World Wide Web. Pop-up windows can present some problems during co-browsing, as can links that cause a new browser window to launch. Co-browsing to password-protected areas of the Web can cause problems and mixed results, too.

Co-browsing to audio and video clips presents certain challenges as well. The online event facilitator cannot know what will happen on each person's computer when the facilitator co-browses to a linked audio or video file. Generally the file will begin to download and each user's media player of choice, such as Windows Media Player, will launch and begin playing the downloaded content.

But because it can be disconcerting to an individual members of your virtual studio audience to suddenly see a file start to download on their computers without them having initiated it (it may be perceived as a virus), rather than co-browse directly to these files, the facilitator may encourage each participant to click on the link unilaterally. That way the decision whether or not to follow the link is left to each individual.

The Library of Congress conducts many wonderful live online programs. Each program provides a glimpse into a small sliver of the massive and varied collections of printed and digital information. Often the programs include digital images, audio clips, and videos. After hosting several online programs, the librarians who present for the Library of Congress decided that is was better to simply point out a link in their digital collections that launched some media file, then let participants decide if they want to click on that link. The presenters would then pause for an appropriate length of time to let the participants experience the media file or explore a small set of media files.

Another thing to note about co-browsing is that it need not be an off/on situation. In some Web conferencing software you, as the organizer or presenter, can allow the participants to browse at will individually. However, as soon as you, the designated co-browser, go somewhere on the Web within the browser embedded in the Web conferencing software, everyone else's embedded browser window will be taken to that Web page, too. By implementing co-browsing in this manner, you can allow individual participants to browse on their own a bit, as long as they understand that as soon as you co-browse somewhere, their individualized wanderings will come to an abrupt end.

Application Sharing

Co-browsing can be thought of as one instance of the general functionality of application sharing, where the moderator or leader is sharing his or her browser screen with everyone else in the room. Application sharing in general is a feature within Web conferencing software that enables everyone in the online room to at least see a shared application (such as word processing or spreadsheet software) from their respective computers in real time. Everyone sees the cursor move and the actions of the application software on the document or the information object. The value of application sharing is that it allows the entire group in the online room to see in its entirety the person's interaction with that application. Every cursor movement, every field in a search engine box that is filled in, every change to a word processing file or spreadsheet is seen by everyone. Application sharing within a live online event or meeting allows a group working on a report or document to see how the changes they are suggesting look and read as they make them. In an online budget meeting, everyone participating in the online meeting can see how the line item changes and scenarios being discussed affect the overall budget picture.

Application sharing also can be an effective way to share with an online group the experience of using a proprietary Web application. Application sharing seems to work much better than simple co-browsing for this purpose, because application sharing "fools" the proprietary Web site into thinking that the information is being sent to only one screen, while in fact it is being sent to many. This is useful, for example, during a workshop when the facilitator wants to show the group a subscription-based information resource or a copy cataloging interface.

Application sharing can also obviate the need to convert and upload content. Rather than save a PowerPoint file as a set of HTML pages, then upload the resulting cluster of files to a server, the presenter can merely share his or her PowerPoint application with the slides in their native format running in real time on the presenter's computer. Animations and other higher order aspects of a fancy PowerPoint presentation may present better in an online meeting environment when application sharing is used, too.

Desktop Sharing

Desktop sharing enables the presenter or facilitator to share his or her entire computer desktop, including all the applications that are open at that time, with the entire group. It can be useful for demonstrations or workshops involving some computing or work process that involves interacting with two or more applications. If a group is working on a report that involves both co-browsing the Web for information as well as writing and editing a document, desktop sharing enables the person in control to toggle between these two applications with ease.

Whiteboarding

A whiteboard in online programming functions like a blackboard or flip chart in a face-to-face program. It allows either a blank slate to be presented to a group, or a preexisting document, such as a word processing document or a spreadsheet, to be loaded so that designated doodlers can scribble on it, highlight and underline key aspects, overlay textual notes, and so on. Your library or library-related organization may want or need to be able to confer whiteboarding powers to selected individuals while they are in an online room. You may also want or need to be able to capture and save the results of a whiteboarding doodle session (for example, if the online session has involved some intense and intricate brainstorming that would be difficult to remember or communicate in some other way).

Most Web conferencing software that contains whiteboarding functionality enables everyone attending the online event to add to the whiteboard. Bell and Shank (2006) describe how they use the group whiteboarding feature to facilitate some ice-breaking and bonding activity at the beginning of an online session. "We always begin a virtual presentation with a map of the United States and then ask our participants, using one of several drawing tools that come with most conferencing software, to indicate where they are on the map. It immediately helps to create a small community out of a disparate group of individuals."

Ease of Learning

The ease with which Web conferencing software can be learned is a subjective experience that may vary from person to person and be difficult to describe and evaluate during the system selection process. Nevertheless, it is a legitimate and vital selection criterion for a Web conferencing system. You want your Web conferencing system to be easily and quickly learned —at least the core functionality—so that new users do not feel disadvantaged in comparison to experienced users of the software. Ultimately, as a program coordinator you want everyone to feel at ease with the Web conferencing system so that they can concentrate on the topic of the online event rather than fumbling around with technical issues. In a similar way, during an in-person event you want the room temperature, lighting, and seating to be comfortable so that people focus on the presenter and the topic.

Ease of Use

Ease of use is related to but different from ease of learning. Once everyone in an online room has become reasonably acclimated to the online meeting environment, you will want to use of the Web conferencing software to be intuitive and easy to use. The availability and intelligibility of online documentation and help may be a factor in ease of use, too.

Omniscience and Omnipotence of the Moderator

The management and control of an online programming service resides principally in the rights and responsibilities of those who have moderator status, as well as in the power and configurability of the administrative module.

In some Web conferencing software systems, the moderator cannot be cognizant of or view private text chat conversations unless he or she is involved in those conversations. In other Web conferencing software systems, the moderator can view these private text chat conversations, and the powers of surveillance are not self-evident to the private text chatters themselves.

Moderators often have the power to interrupt the current speaker, prohibit any or all participants from speaking or engaging in text chat, ban individuals from the room, or prohibit the making of recordings of a session.

When selecting a Web conferencing system, you need to think about how much the moderator may need to know or control about the various facets of an online event. Will the moderator ever need to take over the computer desktops of one or more of the participants in an online event?

Obviously, the nature of the online programs you plan to produce and present will have a bearing on how you will answer these questions. The moderator of a small workshop, for example, with a hefty registration fee and educational credits at stake may need more control over the entire communication and content distribution processes involved in that online event than the moderator of a free online event open to the entire general public.

Administrative Module

Any online meeting room based on a Web conferencing system can be understood as a set of two related rooms: the front room (the parlor) and the back room (the kitchen). The parlor is where you, as the program organizer, meet and entertain your guests. The kitchen is where you keep the broom and mop and gussy up the parlor in general. The administrative module for a Web conferencing system can be understood as the back room where you can configure and control how the front room—the public room —looks and operates. For example, the room management module in the tcConference Web conferencing software enables the room manager to open and close the online room, set and change passwords for moderators and participants, change the default Web page that appears in the embedded browser window when participants enter the online room, change the basic look and feel of the room, enable or disable various functions, change the sound quality, access the room usage statistics, and more.

Usage Reports

You will undoubtedly want to glean usage reports about your online programming service. The two major building blocks of a useful set of usage reports are the statistics provided by the Web conferencing service and those provided by the Web hosting service you select. The usage reports provided by tcConference indicate the names the persons typed in when they entered a room, the IP address they came from, the date and time they entered the room, and the date and time they left the room. If two or more names are input from the same IP address, those names are clustered around that IP address.

Statistics provided by most Web hosting services generally follow the evolving best practices of the Web log analysis software. The Web statistics package within the 1and1 Web hosting package shows the number of page visits (page impressions) during a given period of time, the number of unique visits to your Web site during the specified period of time, the number of pages viewed per visit, referrers (that is, the Web sites that people visited just prior to coming to your Web site), the geographic location of the visitors to your site (rough estimates without much granularity, based on Internet service providers and top level domains), the operating systems and browser software used by visitors to your site, and the number of times each page on your Web site was accessed. You also can download the original log files and run them through your Web log analysis software of choice.

Make sure the usage reports can be output in a form that is most useful to your organization. Ideally, you should be able to export the statistics into spreadsheet software for additional local analysis and manipulation.

Ability to Record and Archive Presentations

The ability to record, archive, and podcast live online events is so important that we've devoted an entire chapter to it (see Chapter 8). Suffice it to say here that the power and flexibility of the recording features vary from one Web conferencing system to the next.

Interoperability with Other Information and Communication Systems

As the manager of an online programming initiative, consider and explore how your online programming platform interacts with other information and communication systems used by your library and/or parent organization. If during the course of an online event you plan to co-browse the virtual studio audience into a password-protected database, be sure your platform can handle it; and test your ability to do this beforehand with colleagues. If you want to integrate your online programming efforts with course management software, be sure to ask plenty of questions of both vendors and test extensively before making a purchase/lease decision for your library or organization. Also, if you plan to show media files during an online event, test how well the Web conferencing system handles the file types you plan to use.

Accessibility

Accessibility is a tremendously complex and nuanced concept. It can and does involve the physical, cognitive, technological, social, and economic abilities of both individuals and groups to access an information resource or a communication system. At the very least, you will want to test the Web conferencing system to learn how accessible it is for blind and low-vision users as well as deaf and hearing-impaired users. Bear in mind that many blind and low-vision users use assistive software (such as Zoomtext, WindowEyes, and JAWS) to either increase the size of text on the screen or to vocalize textual information via text-to-speech technology. For deaf and hearing-impaired users, speech-to-text (speech recognition) software such as Dragon Naturally Speaking can convert spoken audio to visual text on the fly. On the technology accessibility axis, learn which operating systems are supported by the Web conferencing system. Consider also the technical specifications and costs of any computer peripherals (such as headsets and video cameras) that users of the Web conferencing system may be required or strongly encouraged to use.

Reliability

Many of the Web conferencing systems I frequently use appear to be quite reliable. When these systems do fail, sometimes the proximate cause is something beyond the immediate control of the Web conferencing service provider. However, be sure to investigate and inquire about possible problem areas.

Technical Support

Because most Web conferencing systems are hosted services from the vendors, technical support is often provided by the vendors themselves.

The need for live online tech support can be crucial as a library, a library consortium, or a library-related organization hosts a series of live online programs, conferences, and professional development opportunities.

When selecting a Web conferencing system, do not allow the bells and whistles to turn into a siren call. Think about what functions are actually going to be used by your online programming initiative. One time I attended a live online library event, sponsored by a vendor that was using one of the premier—and most expensive—Web conferencing systems on the market. Most of the functionality was not used at all. In fact, some of the functionality had been grayed out. Why pay for what you're never going to use?

FEATURES ANALYSIS

As you investigate Web conferencing software to use for you live online programming service, consider the following features.

Access Levels

Most Web conferencing software systems allow participants in a live online event to have different statuses. In tcConference from Talking Communities three statuses are available: user, moderator, or administrator. Each successive increase in status adds a new set of rights, available functions, and responsibilities. Some Web conferencing systems allow the status of an individual to be changed on the fly while that person is in the online room. Other systems allow changes only beforehand.

Passwords

Most Web conferencing software enables the use of password protection into the online room. Usually either one password can be sent to the entire group that will be coming into the online event, or individual passwords could be assigned to each individual who has been invited or who has registered for an online event. In the OPAL collaborative online programming service that I coordinate, most of the online rooms are usually configured so that all moderators share one password, while regular participants are not required to enter a password. In addition, the fact that moderators and participants can enter any username they wish lessens the burden on each person to remember and use a specific username.

Other Essential Functions for a Successful Online Program

Of all the functionality available through Web conferencing software, it may be useful—if only as a catalyst for discussion and argument—to list the essential functionalities for a successful online library program. These include the following:

Voice-over-IP.—In my opinion, this is the functionality that humanizes the online interaction and differentiates Web conferencing from instant messaging, text chatting, and blogging. It even improves on podcasting a lecture or demonstration because in VoIP there is the potential for true human dialogue.

Text Chatting.—The nature of listening to another person speak requires a mono channel. By that I mean that to be an effective communication only one person should speak at any given time. If two or more people speak at once, a cacophony ensues and the prospects for effective communication decline significantly. Communication via human voice differs from communication via music on this score. If done well, simultaneously listening to two or more instruments being played at once—such as a jazz trio, a rock band, a big band, or an orchestra—is pleasant and communicative. Often the end result is better than the sum of the parts. However, you want to allow all participants to have the opportunity to speak somehow. Text chatting in an online room, therefore, is essential so that everyone else in the online room can communicate while a speaker speaks.

Private Text Chatting.—This function is essential primarily for social reasons, not for pure communication reasons. People get together at public and professional events not only to experience a live lecture, debate, interview, panel discussion, or whatever, but also to chat with colleagues and friends. The private text chat function within Web conferencing software enables this type of back-of-the-lecture-hall and lobby whispering, or passing notes, between two or more individuals.

Follow-Me Browsing.—Synchronized browsing provides the common visual experience for the attendees of a live online event that complements and balances the live audio information being communicated. As Bell and Shank (2006) note, presentation slides (and Web pages) "provide visual stimulation and cues for attendees."

One caution note: people browse much more quickly alone than they should when presenting. When watching someone else browse, members of the virtual studio audience may become dazed and confused. Some ways for you as the presenter to avoid this situation is to slow down as you browse, do your rapid browsing in a separate browser outside of the online room (copying and pasting pertinent URLs into the embedded browser in the online room only when they have been found), or explain orally to the members of the virtual studio audience what you are doing as you co-browse.

Nice But Nonessential Functions for a Successful Online Program

The following functionalities can be considered nice features, but not absolutely essential to a successful online event:

Streaming Video.—The human visage conveys much nonverbal communication. Seeing the speaker's face in real time as he or she speaks can be meaningful and valuable. Although a visual image of the speaker might be great,
being able to see and interact with information objects is a good way to communicate, too.

Keep in mind that talking heads (live videos of the speaker's face or torso)
are not very communicative, interesting, or comforting in the long run—
especially over the course of a one-hour online program. In the same manner, watching crowd activity in a bricks-and-mortar meeting room, lecture
hall, or convention center does not contribute much to the success of an online program, or even the online portion of a combo event (that is, both in
person and online).

Whiteboarding.—Although the ability to write on the screen that consti-
tutes a Web conferencing room can be a nice touch, and even essential in certain situations (such as group brainstorming sessions), generally it is not vital
to a successful online event. People take in visual information presented in
PowerPoint slides and Web pages with amazing alacrity. Unless the presentation slide or Web page is extremely packed or egregiously poorly designed,
there really is little benefit in laser pointing to portions or underlining or cir-
cling things. Five years ago laser pointers were the hot technology for in-
person conference lectures. I personally have not seen one used in the past
two years. In most instances they simply are not needed.

ACCESSIBILITY

Some experts estimate that up to 10 percent of the world's population has
some sort of challenge when trying to access information. The challenge may
involve mobility, blindness or deafness, or other vision or hearing problems.
In nations where the average age is higher—these nations tend to be the
developed nations of the world—the percentage of people with accessibility
challenges are often higher, because incidences of accessibility challenges
generally increase with age. ecause nearly all libraries try to serve all patrons
within their defined core service population, most libraries that are developing and deploying an online programming service need to address the accessibility challenges.

The sad fact is that most creators and vendors of Web conferencing software and systems need to have their consciousness raised on this matter
because their awareness hovers near absolute zero. For example, even
though most Web conferencing systems offer at least two channels of communication—audio and video—many vendors cannot even imagine that a
blind or deaf person would want to participate in a live online event. So,

the vendors do not even consider how information conveyed visually could be co-conveyed audibly, and vice versa.

The good news is that a few vendors are attuned to this challenge and opportunity to make Web conferencing systems accessible to all. Elluminate Live! (www.elluminate.com/accessibility.jsp) identifies three major accessibility challenges in the Web conferencing arena:

- having a system that works on most major computer operating systems, including Microsoft, Mac, and Linux;
- having a system that works well (for all major functionalities, including voice-over-IP and video) across the Internet bandwidth spectrum; and
- having a system that works well for people with physical challenges.

Most Web conferencing vendors are at least aware of the first two accessibility challenges; it's the third one that often proves to be a consciousness-raising challenge.

For the third category, one key accessibility feature is to offer keystroke alternatives for all the buttons and drop-down menus in the Web conferencing environment. Keystroke alternatives make your online meeting room environment much more accessible and functional for blind and visually impaired users of screen reader software programs. In the United States the major screen reader software programs are WindowEyes from GW Micro (www.gwmicro.com/products) and JAWS for Windows from Freedom Scientific (www.freedomscientific.com/fs_products/software_jaws.asp).

Elluminate Live! offers a closed captioning option for the hearing challenged, user control over whether or not one receives an audible sound when certain events occur within an online meeting room, the ability to enlarge the display, and the ability to modify the color scheme for persons who are color blind.

For years Talking Communities (www.talkingcommunities.com) has been another vendor of Web conferencing software and systems known for its accessibility efforts. George Buys, the founder and CEO, is blind, so accessibility features were designed into their system early in the process, not as an afterthought. They provide enhanced accessibility features for persons with vision, hearing, and/or mobility challenges. For example, they have incorporated a text to speech (TTS) engine into their system so that text chat can be made synthetically audible for anyone, not just users of screen reader software. A separate video window for signing also will be made available in future releases.

iVocalize is a third vendor of Web conferencing systems and software that is known to have better than average accessibility for people with vision, hearing, and mobility challenges.

there is no possibility of annoying dual speakers, which often happens during a telephone-based conference call. Most Web conferencing systems also have some mechanism for indicating when a person wishes to speak.

The multiple communication modes of text chatting and voice-over-IP can also improve the efficiency and effectiveness of online meetings and conference calls. The ability to co-browse is another benefit.

Consider also if you want to rent out your online rooms to recognized public groups. For example, the local Kiwanis club may want to rent your online room every Tuesday at 8:00 A.M. for its weekly online meeting.

CONCLUSION

We have found that small, private or semi-private online events often require more functionality from Web conferencing software than do larger public events. As I have attended live in-person presentations at conferences and workshops over the past two decades, I have noticed that presentations that attempt to introduce too many modes of presentation—such as live Internet demonstrations—often do not achieve their objectives. The same is true with live online presentations, especially in front of large online audiences. Keep it simple, relaxed, and lively, and you will hold your online audience much better than if you try to use all the bells and whistles available to you via the Web conferencing system you are using.

As you develop and rollout your online programming initiative, you may want to think about the type of relationship you want to have with your Web conferencing vendor. It could be formal or informal, distant and sporadic or close and frequent, antagonistic or friendly. Even if you opt for an open source Web conferencing system, your library or library-related organization is going to have some sort of relationship with that open source community. If the Web conferencing service you select is large with a large customer base, your ability to have a close, collaborative relationship will likely be diminished. If you select a small Web conferencing software company, they may actively seek your input into how to improve their software and services.

Web conferencing software is so versatile it can be used for some of the "backroom" processes of your online programming service, such as team meetings, internal orientation and training sessions, and recording sessions. When selecting your online programming software, consider carefully your library's needs and the features being offered.

5

Training, Orientation, and Support

CHAPTER SUMMARY

In this chapter you'll find an overview of the various training and orientation modes for helping people become accustomed to and gain ultimate value from an online library programming initiative. In addition, you'll find advice on how to handle problem reports, troubleshooting, and so on.

INTRODUCTION

The goal of training and orientation events and resources supporting a Web conferencing service is to help those who use the service in whatever capacity to feel comfortable within that online environment, and to ensure that they know what functions exist and how to use them so that they can pursue their information or entertainment needs. There is no magic bullet that ensures that the training, orientation, and support services associated with an online programming effort will be successful in all situations. Instead, offer opportunities in a variety of modes, then let participants choose the modes that best fit their needs and learning styles.

The basic getting started guide can be offered as a text document in a variety of file formats (such as HTML, PDF, or Microsoft Word). A basic getting started session could be offered periodically as an online event in its own right. Essentially, you offer to meet people online to help them get acclimated to online events and the Web conferencing systems that make online events possible. If you do offer online getting started sessions, they can be recorded and archived so that others can access the information conveyed in the online session at any time.

You also can use desktop video software such as Camtasia to create canned screen videos of the processes involved in getting started with and using your online service and the Web conferencing system you have selected to power the service. Different versions of these screen videos can be created to meet the specific needs and interests of the general public, people who will be presenters, people who will serve as online room managers, and so on.

Installing client software and providing access to a Web conferencing system in a local area network can result in many requests for technical support. This may be a situation where your best move as the service coordinator is merely to put the IT people at the library or library-related organization in contact with the technical support staff at the Web conferencing service you have selected.

PREPARING THE PARTICIPANTS

The single most effective way to train librarians and end-users alike to lead or participate in an online event is to get them into an online room, let them look around, and engage in some basic trial-and-error learning. Usually within a few minutes the user feels fairly comfortable in the online room. Achieving a basic comfort level is the key hurdle to overcome. Once users feel comfortable in the room, they can learn advanced features at their own pace as the need or interest arises. If they do not become comfortable, it probably will produce a negative halo effect about their overall estimation of the value of online events and Web conferencing.

An online orientation session can also be recorded and archived, so that people can access the orientation session on their own time schedules. That enables them to pause the playback, test a feature, take notes, ponder what was just said, and so on.

An audio recording, perhaps delivered as a podcast, can be another effective way to provide basic orientation. The person can listen to the orientation while exploring a test online room on their own.

Ideally, orientation to the Web conferencing online environment should occur in an online room. Experiencing the online room is a much more efficient and effective instructional experience than any PowerPoint presentation, screen video, or getting started guide. When you try to explain in words and pictures how Web conferencing software and an online room works, peoples' eyes glaze over rather quickly. But when they are actually in an online room and have the features and functionality demonstrated to them (with ample opportunities to play with the functionality), their interest level remains high and they learn quickly.

Basic, intermediate, and advanced forms of orientation should be provided for members of the virtual studio audience, for speakers and facilitators of online events, and for managers and tech support people of online events (including orientation to the administrative module and how to upload presentations).

Offering a recorded and archived version of an orientation session is the next best thing to attending an actual live online demonstration. As the manager of an online programming initiative, you can simply record one of the live online orientation sessions you offer periodically, or you can go into an unused online room with no virtual studio audience present and use the room basically as a recording studio.

In preparation for the Day of the Digital Audio Book that LibraryU and OPAL co-sponsored in February 2006, we offered several online sessions prior to the big day, when registrants could come into the room, test the microphone and speaker connections, and learn about how the online room and online event would work in general. Although only a small percentage of the total number of registrants attended any one of these preparation sessions, those who did appreciated them.

Because orientation information and materials can quickly become out of date or simply in need of revision, expansion, or contraction, based on feedback you receive from people who use the orientation materials, keep the materials—both print-based and recorded—broken up into small, discrete segments. Then, as each segment becomes outdated, update that segment, which is much more manageable than overhauling all of your training and orientation documentation.

When providing an online orientation session, be sure to have a good, well-organized outline for the session. Sometimes a getting started guide can be used as an outline, with the presenter highlighting and glossing what he or she considers to be the especially important points. Be prepared, however, to abandon your outline temporarily or permanently if your group becomes engaged and asks lots of questions. It is better to tailor on the fly your online orientation session to meet the needs and interests of the actual members of the virtual studio audience than to plow through a planned presentation.

Orientation and training sessions have two basic goals. First, you want to ensure that the user is able to download and install the client software, if necessary, to be able to enter the online room, to hear voice communication emanating from the room, and to use the software's audio input device. This process is similar to downloading and installing any software and beginning to use any new piece of hardware. People need to get it up and working before they can actually begin learning how to use it. This first goal can be a considerable source of frustration for users, especially if they already conceptually understand and appreciate the power of Web conferencing systems and online events. As the program coordinator, you should offer some other means of communication (such as a phone number, email address, or a Twitter account) where users can reach you as they try to achieve this first goal.

Unfortunately, it can be very difficult to troubleshoot from a distance any installation problems that may arise. Getting the voice-over-IP functionality to work can be particularly nettlesome. Patience is required of everyone involved. Using telephones to communicate during these early stages of use is not forbidden and should not be perceived as a sign of failure.

Because audio input and output can be two frequent areas of problems, many Web conferencing services offer online ways to test these functions before the person actually enters the room.

When considering the differences between a live in-person event and a live online event, the organizers and presenters are merely swapping one set of anxieties for another. For an in-person event, attendees are being asked to suspend their normal work lives and travel to a gathering point that often is unfamiliar (or only vaguely familiar) to them. For some people who attend live in-person events, the opportunity to get away from the office and one's normal routine may be a prime motivator for attending; for others, it is a hassle. The walls often are bare, the chairs are straight-backed, the coffee is weak, and the pastries are stale. The microphone may not work, the computer may not be in the room—the list goes on. All of these factors can create performance anxiety for the speaker. The speaker is being asked to stand in front of a group of people and make them conclude that leaving one's home and usual haunts, traveling to a sensory deprivation chamber, and turning one's attention to the speaker and the topic was worth the time, trouble, and expense.

A speaker at a live online event must confront a different set of anxieties. Most people attend live online events from their work areas. Because a computer is required to participate in a live online event, and because computers are the great enabler of multitasking, the speaker may have a difficult time gaining and holding the attention of the virtual studio audience. Added to that is the anxiety of not really knowing if you, the speaker, have gained and held the attention of your audience. Usually in an online meeting space, you cannot visually scan the audience, look in their eyes, and make sure they are paying attention.

PREPARING LIBRARIANS AND LIBRARY STAFF MEMBERS AT THE PARTICIPATING LIBRARY OR LIBRARIES

When providing training, orientation, and support for other librarians, you can be a little more detailed in the information you provide. Some librarians may be interested primarily in the programs you are offering online, rather than the underlying technology and the functionality of the software per se. Other librarians may be interested in how your online programming service operates as a service organization. Still others may be interested in the specific Web conferencing system you have selected, while some may be interested primarily in Web conferencing systems as a product category. Each and all of these various interests may be expressed directly or indirectly during online training and orientation sessions. As the trainer or orientation guide, be attuned to the possibility of these varying needs and respond accordingly.

PREPARING PROGRAM PRESENTERS

When providing online training and orientation sessions for people who already know they will be online presenters themselves in the near future, you can be fairly certain that you will have a highly motivated virtual studio audience. These presenters may arrive at the orientation session with preconceived misconceptions about what will be required of them as presenters. However, their anxiety about presenting may make them impatient during your online orientation session. Because of this, it is usually best to let members of the virtual studio audience interrupt and ask questions at any time during your orientation presentation, rather than at designated Q&A pauses.

Many presenters in online programs initially think that it will be more difficult and anxiety-inducing to present online as opposed to in person. This attitude may flip-flop soon. Many presenters may begin to *prefer* presenting online, rather than in person. One reason for this is that they have more presentation and communication modes available to them. Another reason is that they are busy people and want to use their time efficiently. Some presenters really enjoy presenting from their homes, with their bunny slippers on and their pets at their sides. (Several times in the past few years I have heard dogs woof in the background as people speak during online events, including my own dog, Max.)

Your primary goal when providing training and orientation for presenters is to make them comfortable with the technology so that they can concentrate on delivering their presentation and interacting with the online virtual studio audience. Some presenters who are fantastic at live in-person presentations are not so great as live online presenters. Other presenters who may be self-conscious or disjointed in front of an in-person group feel relaxed and strangely liberated when presenting online; their voice becomes more relaxed and engaging when they present online.

Because the speaker's voice is the primary form of communication during many live online programs, as the event coordinator be sure to test the presenter's audio before the actual start of the event. As Bell and Shank (2006) note, "A virtual presenter enters a rather strange world. After our initial sessions we shared a renewed appreciation for nonverbal communication, and we've heard this from the many colleagues who've been participants." Make sure that your presenter's voice is not too soft or too loud. Also make sure that their mouth is not too close to the microphone, which may make them sound breathy and cause certain vocal sounds to aspirate.

As discussed previously, online events can involve more audience participation—some of which may be instigated by the presenter, and some of which will undoubtedly be unsanctioned—which can be distracting to the presenter. For example, if a virtual studio audience is particularly chatty, the scrolling text chat banter may be distracting to the presenter. Some presenters may choose to ignore or even hide the text chat. Or, one of the event facilitators can monitor the text chat, watching for good questions and comments to repeat during planned Q&A segments of the online presentation.

The participatory aspect of Web conferencing software is one of its strengths. Bell and Shank (2006) quote Dan Balzar's thoughts on how to exploit this strength: "the most effective way to honor the participants' time is to engage them in concrete, practical activities such as skill development, project design, or brainstorming."

PREPARING MEMBERS OF THE VIRTUAL STUDIO AUDIENCE

Online programming should be about content and group interaction, not about technology (unless some technology is the topic of the online program, of course). The goal, therefore, is to get each member of the virtual studio audience acclimated to the online Web conferencing environment as quickly as possible. Some members of the virtual studio audience may have attended previous online events and feel comfortable with the entire situation. Others may need some quick tutorials provided on-the-fly. Most Web conferencing service providers offer online documentation, tutorials, and training videos, but often they tend to be rather generic and may not address a specific set of functions based upon how you have configured your online room and set the various permissions. The minutes leading up to the official start of an online event are a good time to field questions and show people the basic functionality.

CONCLUSION

Training, orientation, and technical support activities will be ongoing components of any live online programming service you undertake. New users will be attending the online events you plan and present, infrequent users will need refreshers, and software and system upgrades will change how things are accomplished for all users. You will want to work closely with your Web conferencing service provider, the staff at your library (especially the IT staff), and the other member organizations of your consortium (if you are involved in a consortial initiative) to ensure that regular participants, presenters, event facilitators, and others have access to current training information in a variety of formats.

6

Promotional Efforts

CHAPTER SUMMARY

This chapter summarizes effective ways to announce and promote online library programs, including both individual programs and the service as a whole.

INTRODUCTION

You do not need to spend much money to have an effective and efficient promotional campaign for your online programs. In this age of massive email discussion lists, social networks, free blogs, podcasts, video sharing sites, and other Web 2.0 tools, it is relatively easy to get the word out about upcoming programs. Getting your message to a rather well-defined population, such as librarians, however, is much easier than getting your message out to the entire population of a specific geographic area—or, in the case of a global programming effort, the world. The general public receives so many promotional messages that attempt to capture their attention and get them to commit their time (and, usually, their money) that your lowly message about free library-sponsored online programs may become lost in the welter. Even in this age of multiple free and easy to use online tools for promotion, a little strategy and forethought can help.

When planning a promotional campaign, think initially in broad terms. The major factors in a promotional campaign include the timing of the

promotional messages (do you want your message to be waiting in everyone's email inbox first thing in the morning, or do you want it to arrive during the day on weekdays?), the formats of the promotional messages
(textual, audio, video), the channels for the promotional messages (email,
blogs, wikis, Facebook, Twitter, YouTube), the content of the messages (just
the facts, humorous, winsome), and the frequency of the messages. For
example, think how irritating is it when the same TV commercial plays
two or more times on the same channel during an hour of television viewing.
Most people have a very low tolerance for listening to or viewing a commercial or announcement two or more times in a relatively short time span.

Publicizing upcoming online events is a major challenge for any online
library public programming initiative. If people are not made aware of the
public online event you are planning, there is absolutely no chance they will
attend. The goal is to push out information about upcoming programs in a
way that is informative to—and appreciated by—the target audience without annoying anyone. This is a perpetual challenge, because contradictory
needs are apparent within the general population interested in online
programming.

Some people want to be notified as soon as possible about upcoming online events. They put these events on their calendars, then forget about them
until the day of the scheduled online event. Others want to be reminded of
an upcoming online event as close to the event as possible. This segment of
the population seems to understand attending an online event as a spur of
the moment decision. They seem to be saying: If you remind me of this event
as close to its start time as possible, and if I'm available and interested in
attending, then I may attend. Another segment of the population seems to
want it both ways. They want both a preliminary announcement as far in
advance of the online event as possible, plus a last-minute reminder. Clearly,
promotional efforts that try to meet the needs and preferences of one group
may actually annoy another group and disincline them to attend.

Some people prefer to have announcements pushed out to them. You may
want to offer an easy-to-subscribe-to email announcement list or RSS (really
simple syndication) feed, so that people can self-select to receive these types
of pushed announcements. If you create an announcement email list, be sure
to use it sparingly and only for announcements about upcoming programs
and major changes to the service. Podcasting brief promotional audio
recordings is one way to achieve this, because each individual decides to subscribe to the online program's feed.

KNOW YOUR AUDIENCE

The audience for online public programs can be divided into two categories: those who attend the live online event and those who access and use

the recorded and archived live online events. As we noted above, the live audience can be thought of as the virtual studio audience, or perhaps the synchronous audience. They are the ones who get the opportunity to contribute to the conversation and the overall value and success of the online event. The users of the archive are the time-shifters as well as place-shifters. They access a previously recorded online program when and where they want. The trade-off for them, of course, is that they cannot contribute in a meaningful way with the conversation. They are like readers of a book, or a newspaper, or even of a blog. They can write a review of the book, write a letter to the newspaper editor, or post a comment to a blog entry, but their opportunity to influence and participate in the initial warp and woof of the live online event lies petrified in the past. They know this, and are willing to accept this trade-off for the benefit of being able to listen to and view an online program whenever they want.

ONLINE MARKETING IDEAS FROM SARAH HOUGHTON-JAN

In May 2008 Sarah Houghton-Jan, the Digital Futures Manager (great position title) at the San Jose, California Public Library provided a very informative OPAL online program about online marketing strategies and tools for libraries (www.opal-online.org/houghtonjan20080508). She focused on free and low-cost online marketing approaches. The goal of any library marketing effort is to connect potential users with the services and staff they need to advance their information lives. Houghton-Jan notes that in the online environment, every user is potentially a user of your library's online programs. You may try to reach your core clientele, but your online promotional efforts will and should reach many other potential participants in your online programs. She recommends that your library or online program be listed in at least the top four online directories:

- AskCity
- Yahoo! Local
- Google Maps, and
- Microsoft Live Search Maps.

Note that you can "beef up" many of these online directory resources with photos, reviews, and more.

Houghton-Jan also notes that libraries and online programs should be listed in at least the five top library directories:

- LibDex: The Library Index,
- LibWeb,
- MapMuse,

- PublicLibraries.com, and
- Libraries411.com.

If you want to purchase online advertisements for your Web conferencing service in general or for specific online events, you can buy online ads through Google AdWords, Yahoo! Smart ads, Microsoft adCenter, and other online advertisers.

To reach your library's core clientele as defined in your library's mission statement, Houghton-Jan recommends listing your library's events and services in one or more local community Web sites and calendars, such as AmericanTowns.com, Upcoming.org, Eventful, Craigslist, YourEventHub.com, ImThere.com, Going.com, Down2Night.com, BusyTonight.com, and LibraryThing Local. You can also send online event announcements to other local organizations and encourage them to promulgate these announcements on their Web sites and email distribution lists.

Another suggestion, based on a comment by Michael Stephens, is that libraries create entries for themselves and their online programming efforts in Wikipedia. Be sure that the library is mentioned in other pertinent Wikipedia entries, such as the entry for your town, college, school district, and so on.

Overall, the idea is that you develop an online marketing plan with a budget containing dollars, staff hours, and other needed resources. Begin with the easy-to-do things that do not require updating and maintenance. This is the best way to get the biggest bang for your marketing investment. Then move on to online marketing strategies that require ongoing maintenance. Remember to configure your announcements so that they can be reused in different marketing channels with minimal reformatting and effort. Add reminders to maintain all these channels to your personal calendar as a recurring event.

YOUR WEB SITE AS PART OF YOUR PROMOTIONAL EFFORT

One useful way to list upcoming online events is in chronological order, of course. Having a master calendar that displays all upcoming online events is worthwhile, but breaking the upcoming events out into categories, such as literary events, technology training, and interviews, also helps people find programs of interest to them.

Your Web site itself is a wonderful promotional tool for your online programs, as well as your archive. For example, in 2008 there were over 36,000 visits to the calendar pages on the OPAL Web site. Be sure to keep your Web site up to date with announcements of forthcoming online events.

EMAIL ANNOUNCEMENTS TO INDIVIDUALS AND GROUPS

Sending announcements via electronic mail to email discussion groups and individuals can be a very effective way to promote upcoming online events. Most people at least scan the subject lines of all their incoming email, if for no other reason than to winnow out the spam. Another nice feature of email is that, if the recipient is interested in the announcement, he or she may forward it to friends, family members, and colleagues who may be interested in the announcement, too. This is an instance of virtual word-of-mouth group awareness raising. In the marketing world, it is generally referred to as viral marketing.

Actually, viral marketing is an important component of how people really learn about online events, even if viral marketing is not part of your official marketing strategy. InvestorWords (www.investorwords.com/5251/viral _marketing.html) defines viral marketing as "A marketing tactic relying upon some aspect of the system to cause the promotion to propagate itself as the initial targets pass the promotion onto others. One example of viral marketing is encouraging current and potential customers to tell others about the company's products and services, and in turn encouraging those others to tell even more others."

When we ask attendees to OPAL online events how they heard about an event, often they mention email discussion groups to which announcements were never sent, so they must have been forwarded by others as secondary or tertiary announcements.

One way to encourage viral marketing activity is to include a statement in the promotional message that actively encourages recipients of the message to forward it to others who may be interested in the online program being publicized. The active encouragement to forward the message serves as a gentle reminder to the recipient to consider—however fleetingly—other colleagues, friends, or family members who may be interested in attending the online event.

AN ANNOUNCEMENTS LIST

Having a separate email distribution list for announcements only concerning upcoming programs and service developments is a good idea. Because most people are overwhelmed by the volume of email messages they receive daily (especially when spam messages are factored into the equation), they will welcome a focused, low-volume announcements-only email list. As the coordinator of the promotional effort for your online programming initiative, you need to respect that implicit social contract, and not send too many messages through the announcements list.

BRIEF PODCASTS

As the manager of an online program service, use one of your online rooms as a virtual recording studio to create brief audio recordings and streaming media promotional announcements, then podcast the MP3 version of the audiorecording through the same channels that you use to podcast archived recordings of actual online programs. Links to these audio, streaming media, and screencasts can be placed on the Web site for your online programming service, for those who prefer to grab promotional information rather than have it pushed out to them on a regular basis. For the OPAL online programming initiative, generally we record these types of announcements monthly.

BLOGS

Blogs are another good way to announce upcoming online events. Make sure your blog's RSS feed gets submitted to the major blog search engines. Sarah Houghton-Jan (2008) suggests Feed Submitter as an easy way to submit your feed to multiple sites. Sending personal messages to prominent bloggers in a profession or topical area may yield some good blog posts from them about the value of this upcoming online event. Program presenters and interviewees also may want to add announcements of the online programs to their blogs. Microblogging tools such as Twitter can also be used to announce specific online events.

BRIEF VIDEO ANNOUNCEMENTS

Brief video announcements about your online programming service in general or about specific online events can be made and easily uploaded to YouTube, BlipTV, TeacherTube, and other video sharing sites. Early in 2009 we began experimenting with a very informal, low-budget YouTube video monthly announcement of upcoming programs. After our initial YouTube announcement had been available for one week, it had received over 150 views, which encourages us to continue this method of promulgating announcements.

IN-PERSON TALKS AT CONFERENCES

Managers and promoters of online programming services should not eschew exclusively in-person events, such as conferences, workshops, and annual meetings. These can be good opportunities to acclimate groups to the experience, attractions, and benefits of online programming. Promoting the entire service, rather than a specific online event, probably makes more sense when speaking at a conference or workshop.

CONSORTIAL PROGRAMS AND INDIVIDUAL LIBRARY PROMOTIONAL CHANNELS

If you are involved in an online programming service that is consortial or collaborative in some way, involving two or more libraries or library-related organizations, remember that many of these organizations have their own promotional channels and systems already in place. These may include email distribution lists, podcasts, printed newsletters, Web sites, and other channels. When using the promotional networks already in place at member organizations, you may need to obtain permission to use those channels, design and deliver the message in a generic way and in a flexible format so that the participating organizations can edit the message to meet their "house style," add organization-specific logos or message content, and more. Be sure to add more lead time into your promotional efforts so that your message can be added into these other promotional streams for a timely delivery of the message to the final recipients.

OTHER LIBRARIES AND SERVICES AS PROMOTIONAL VENUES

If your online programming service offers free online programs for library users worldwide, and if non-member libraries are free to point to and promote your online events, some people may wonder what are the advantages to an organization in actually joining the programs, rather than just pointing their patrons to these programs. There is a fundamental disingenuousness—some would call it freeloading—involved in this organizational course of action. Plus the library or other organization has no control over the program selection and development, the governance of the program, or its development. OPAL in general encourages non-member libraries, other online programming services, and other library-related programs to announce upcoming OPAL programs and point their clientele to previous programs in the OPAL archive.

One interesting situation arose in December 2005. A for-profit online information aggregator in a certain topical area contacted the OPAL collaborative asking if they could provide deep links to certain archived programs on that topic. Because they were a for-profit company, in some small way they were asking to use archived OPAL programs to make money through subscriptions to their Web site. At that time, the OPAL project team decided not to encourage that for-profit company to provide deep links to archived OPAL online events.

PROMOTING THE ONLINE PROGRAMS OF OTHER SERVICES

If a library or other organization is truly interested in providing "open source" access to live and previously recorded programs, they may be interested in announcing and promoting programs being created and presented by other organizations and initiatives. For example, your online programming effort may want to enter into some sort of loose, informal arrangement whereby you list all or selected online programs from another online programming effort on your schedule and in your promotional messages. Be sure to ask permission of the leaders of the other online programming efforts before doing this, and be aware that such practices, if used frequently, could result in some "brand confusion" on the part of participants.

WAYS TO DETERMINE WHICH PROMOTIONAL EFFORTS BRING PEOPLE TO ONLINE EVENTS

One way to determine which of your promotional efforts is reaching potential attendees is to ask them. During that awkward period before the official beginning of an online event, when people are in the room but nothing organized is happening, someone from the team that organized the event can simply ask the members of the virtual studio audience to type into text chat how they heard about the program about to begin.

Another way to obtain this information is to examine the Web server logs for announcements that are made available through the project Web site. For example, during the month of January 2006, the streaming audio version of an announcement of upcoming OPAL programs placed on the Web site early in the month was accessed 197 times. The WMA (Windows media audio) version was accessed 113 times. The MP3 version of the five-minute announcement—the version that also was podcast—was accessed 51 times over the course of the month. All told, the three versions of this brief announcement were accessed over 350 times.

REGISTRATION AND PASSWORD ACCESS OPPORTUNITIES

If you offer an online event that is free but requires registration, early evidence indicates that approximately 50–75 percent of those who register will actually attend the live online event. At the inaugural Let's Go Library Expo in late July 2005, 280 people registered and approximately 170 people attended actually attended (60 percent). At the inaugural Library Journal Web cast in the URLearning series held on November 15, 2005, approximately 550 people registered and approximately 350 (64 percent) attended. For a February 2009 free online workshop about audio description, 46 people registered and 40 (87 percent) attended.

THE VALUE OF REGULARLY SCHEDULED PROGRAMS

The Johnson County Library in suburban Kansas City has experimented with having an online program on the first Friday of every month at 10 A.M. Central Time. It is a monthly interview show with Jessa and James, bug artists. The Library of Congress also has a monthly online event on the third Wednesday of each month at the same time. This practice seems to encourage repeat attendance.

CONCLUSION

Promoting online programs to the general public can be very difficult. As Hampton Stevens, a writer and OPAL presenter, once said, to reach the public, you need to try 500 channels of communication. If 500 do not work, try 501. Create your promotional content so that it can be reused in a variety of channels, both the channels that you use and channels that recipients may want to use to forward your announcement.

Promoting online programs to librarians is much easier, because messages sent to a few key email discussion lists are then forwarded to others who the recipients assume may be interested in the program.

When it comes to announcements and a calendar for live online events, what we ultimately need is a master calendar for online programs from a wide variety of libraries, library-related organizations, and collaborative efforts. A basic set of announcement elements—akin to Dublin Core's metadata records for digital objects—would list things such as the title of the event, the presenter, the organizing organization, any sponsors, the topics of the online event (using both a controlled vocabulary and uncontrolled tags), and a standard way of presenting the start time in a way that would be understandable to all potential participants in all time zones around the world; this would be useful to everyone. It would also help avoid interservice scheduling conflicts, which are already cropping up as a problem in the online programming field.

7

Beyond the One-Shot,
One-Hour Online Event

CHAPTER SUMMARY

Although a rich variety of online library programming can be offered easily and efficiently through a collaborative effort among several libraries, in this basic scenario each event essentially stands on its own. This chapter explores ways for you to successfully move beyond a series of one-shot online events. It is possible to hold successful online symposia, workshops, and conferences that span one day, several days, or that are spread over several weeks.

INTRODUCTION

Live online events that last an hour or less have proven popularity, convenience, and impact. For online library programming initiatives, questions will inevitably be raised about whether integrated series of longer, online programs would prove beneficial. Also, some may ask whether people are willing to sit through a one-day online workshop or conference, even if frequent breaks are interspersed.

SERIES OF EVENTS

One way to move your online public programming initiative beyond the one-shot, one-hour event is to offer a series of related programs that preferably occur, for example, on the same day of each month or the same day and time each week. Attendees can then make an ongoing commitment to the series. A monthly online book discussion group focused on a particular time period, author, or genre qualifies as a series of related events. So does a monthly or weekly interview series or informal online salon event. For several years the Henry Morrison Flagler Museum in Florida has been offering a series of thematically related Whitehall Lectures about some aspect of the Gilded Age in America. The lectures always begin on Sunday afternoons at 3:00 Eastern and are held both in person at the museum and online. The combination of a common theme (in 2009 the theme was sports legends of the Gilded Age) and a common start time has resulted in a number of repeat online attendees.

WORKSHOPS

Workshops are another way to attempt to move beyond the one-shot, one-hour online event. A workshop often tries to instill in the participants some sort of practical knowledge, such as how to copy catalog in the OCLC Online Computer Library Center system, or tips and techniques for preparing one's federal and state income tax returns. The emphasis of a workshop, as the name implies, is on work, not on the entertainment value of the presentation, or even on sharing straight information. During a workshop, the relationship between the presenter and the members of the virtual studio audience tends toward the basic relationship between an instructor and a set of pupils.

An online workshop, like an in-person workshop, assumes a high level of interest, commitment, and sustained attention from the workshop participants. This enables the workshop organizers and presenters to break through the one-hour online fatigue barrier. Because of the complex, often detailed information that needs to be conveyed during a typical workshop, more than one hour of online interaction is usually needed. A workshop should take no more and no less time than is needed to convey the material to be covered. Of course, with an online workshop, attendees avoid the travel time to and from the workshop location, which for in-person workshops often turns a three- or four-hour workshop into a day-long or overnight time commitment

Because workshops have special needs and dynamics, they place additional demands on the organizers and presenters of these types of online events—and on the Web conferencing systems that support them. For example, the need to register for a workshop is much more common than for public lectures. Space may be limited, not so much because of the limitations of the Web conferencing software or the contractual agreement between the Web conferencing hosting service and the organizers of the online workshop, but because of the need to keep the group relatively small so that the presenter and the workshop attendees can interact and have a productive, fruitful workshop. In February 2009, I conducted an online 2.5-hour workshop on the topic of audio description, a method of writing descriptions about visual images, then creating audio recordings of the written descriptions so that blind and low-vision individuals can get a sense of the visual images. I had previously given the workshop many times in-person, usually to groups of ten or fewer. For the online workshop, 46 people registered and over 40 actually attended. Because of the large group size, we had to rethink or curtail a couple of interactive writing and recording activities.

Often with the need for registration comes the need for access controls into the online room where the workshop will be held. A password may be created for the entire group of workshop registrants, or individual passwords can be generated for and assigned to individual attendees. Because workshops often require lots of preparation and contact time from an expert in the topic area of the workshop, the organizers may need to charge a registration fee to help recoup the costs of holding the conference, and to give the presenter an honorarium. While many authors, professionals, and experts are willing to speak online for 30 to 45 minutes without receiving an honorarium (the avoidance of the need to travel is very appealing to most of them), few are willing to plan, organize, and present a multi-hour online workshop without receiving some sort of monetary compensation.

The online workshop modes of communicating and sharing information can put special demands on the Web conferencing system itself. The presenter will probably need to exercise dynamically several forms of controlling the flow of the workshop. Follow-me browsing will likely need to be turned on and off frequently. The ability of workshop participants to text-chat, speak using voice-over-IP, be seen via the streaming video from webcams, and other modes of communication will also need to be carefully controlled. In short, no one expects a workshop to be an online free-for-all that some online public events tend to become.

It is possible to offer continuing education (CE) credits for live online workshops. As the workshop organizer, you will need to work with the state (or, alas, states) from which the attendees seeking CE credits hail, then complete the necessary paperwork to become authorized to grant CE credits. State libraries can provide information about how the process works in a particular state.

CONFERENCES

Web conferencing software can be an easy and effective way to offer a conference experience to people. You can have keynote addresses, concurrent sessions, panel discussions, breakout sessions, vendor exhibits, and even social events. When planned well, both one-day and multi-day online conferences can be resounding successes. If the Web conferencing software you use has a versatile recording function, it will probably be easy to capture and archive all of the online conference events, too.

It is not only possible but also easy to offer sponsors and exhibitors online rooms during your conference. Exhibitors can use the online rooms to offer online demonstrations of their products and services, or they could use them for informal conversations with the online conference attendees who stop by to chat.

When I stop by a vendor exhibit at an in-person conference, I often have several purposes. I may be stopping by to meet with a specific representative. Sometimes I have an appointment to meet with that person; sometimes I don't. Or I may wish to speak with any representative about what's new in general with that company or organization, or to learn more about a specific product or service. Or I may be "just browsing"—looking to review their literature and canned demonstrations without really interacting with any human representative of the company. Sometimes I just want to pick up a piece of candy.

Online vendor exhibits may do a better job than in-person exhibits in enabling these different purposes—except the candy giveaway. If a person just wants to examine the wares without speaking or interacting with any company representative, the entryway to the actual online room can serve this purpose. During the inaugural Let's Go Library Expo in the summer of 2005, the entryway of OverDrive, one of the sponsors, was designed specifically to meet the various needs of people who stop by the virtual exhibit space.

There are other advantages of online conferences compared to in-person conferences. The conference organizers need not worry about local arrangements, such as attractive rates for blocks of hotel rooms at locations close to the conference space, travel delays, bad weather, or good weather (which may cause some conference attendees to head outside to see the local sights or go shopping). With an online conference, if you underestimate or overestimate the size of room needed for a particular online session, you can usually adjust the size of the room on the fly.

Compared to in-person conferences, online conferences also often are much less expensive, both for the conference organizers and the individual attendees. Online conferences are more energy efficient, as well, in this era when most organizations are striving to reduce their carbon footprints and become more green.

Another huge advantage of online conferences over in-person conferences is a drastically reduced conference preparation time. An online conference can be created and organized in a couple of months, if not weeks, which is unthinkable for an in-person conference, because meeting space, hotel rooms, and airline reservations must be reserved. This inherent advantage of online conferences over in-person conferences may lead to a lot of online conferences that focus on hot, quickly emerging topics.

For one-day online conferences, scheduling is a challenge. If your target audience is librarians and/or users in the United States, you probably will not want to begin the conference before 11 A.M. Eastern Time, because that is 8 A.M. Pacific Time. (Alaska and Hawaii are the outliers here, both geographically and temporally.) The conference should conclude by 5 P.M. Eastern Time. This gives you a six-hour window for programming. My experience has been that each individual session at a conference should not last much more than 60 minutes. Rather than have back-to-back sessions in one online room, you should set up a sufficient number of rooms so that all online sessions are staggered. For example, online events in Room A could begin at the top of the odd numbered hours (11, 1, and 3), while online events in Room B could begin at the top of even numbered hours (noon, 2, and 4). By scheduling the conference in this way, people entering the online room for the next session will not disrupt the conclusion of the current session. Also, if the first session runs a little more than one hour, the presenters will not feel that they need to cut the discussion short in order to make room for the next presentation. If individual members of the virtual studio audience need to leave at the top of the hour to attend another session in another room, so be it. If people are attending an online conference from multiple time zones, there is really no need and no sense in taking a lunch break. Attendees will eat, take rest room breaks, and other essentials of life on their own.

Having such a packed schedule during a one-day conference, however, can be fatiguing for conference attendees and organizers alike. One way to address the online meeting fatigue problem is to build some downtime into the one-day conference schedule. Also, having a no-conflict time to attend online vendor exhibits and demonstrations will improve traffic to that aspect of your online conference. The Day of the Digital Audio Book one-day conference conducted inn February 2006 as a collaborative effort between LibraryU and OPAL used this downtime strategy to good effect. While online conference organizers may worry that any downtime during the conference may cause attendees to log off and not return, that has not been my experience. Most attendees appreciate the opportunity to attend to offline work and family-related matters during the breaks in the online conference schedule.

There are certain aspects of in-person conferences that simply cannot be replicated online. There is no way to get together with friends for dinner or drinks, nor is there the thrill of visiting a new city or region of the country or world. The chance but fruitful encounters between two or more conference goers as they crisscross the geographic location surrounding the conference center are difficult or impossible to recreate online.

Are there any aspects of online conferences that cannot (or cannot easily) be replicated in an in-person conference? Although the convenience and low cost of attending an online conference may be two of its strongest selling

points, there are others. Internet-based demonstrations at in-person conferences still are not often extremely useful and elegant. The connectivity in
many meeting rooms and conference centers can be cause for trepidation
and loathing, and the screens and monitors in individual assembly rooms
often are difficult to see from all points in the room. Audio delivered over
the Internet often suffers miserably during the "last mile" out into the ears
of the audience in a conference meeting room. It's not uncommon to see
some presenter holding a lavaliere microphone down close to the puny,
tinny audio output from some laptop in a vain attempt to project the audio
output from the Web out into an in-person audience. So, it seems safe to
say that, in general, group exploration of the Web is better in most online
meeting spaces than in most in-person meeting spaces.

Another way online beats in-person is in recording a session. In many Web
conferencing systems anyone in attendance can make a recording that
includes all the essential components of the online group interaction, such
as text chat, audio, and co-browsing. The recording of live in-person presentations and discussions at workshops and conferences still tends to require
rather expensive equipment, even if only the audio track is being recorded.
For that and other reasons, the responsibility for recording live in-person
events at workshops and conferences still resides with the conference organizers or their designees. Because the costs are still rather high, or because the
selling of recorded sessions is seen as a revenue center for the conference
organizers, individuals often have to pay to obtain copies of recorded live
in-person sessions. Individual conference attendees who take it upon themselves to record a session may be met with suspicion at best, open hostility
from the conference organizers at worst. In most Web conferencing systems,
however, it is possible to empower all participants of a live online event to
record the session, as long as all the speakers and participants have been
informed that such recording activity may occur. In this era of Twitter,
instantaneous blogging, Flip video recordings, and a camera in just about
every cell phone (if not a chicken in every pot), almost all speakers and
conference attendees accept (if not embrace) the reality that any in-person
conference is going to be captured and disseminated in many ways by many
people. The same attitude seems to hold for online conferences as well.

At in-person conferences, the informal discussions in hallways, foyers, restaurants, and watering holes are often as informative and useful to
conference goers as are the formal presentations and discussions. Unfortunately, it is difficult to replicate the myriad, often serendipitous, opportunities for networking in the online meeting room environment. At various
online workshops and conferences I have seen attempts at virtual coffee
houses (bring your own coffee), pre-event spaces such as lobbies, and happy
hours (bring your own happiness), but in general they do not work well and
are not well attended. People don't mind coming into an online room for a
specific online event, but most people don't seem inclined to come into an

online room just to hang out with others and talk about whatever comes to mind. Without the actual presence of other human bodies, food, and drink, this does not work well. However, attendees of online workshops and conferences do like to chat informally before and after (and sometimes during, to the chagrin of the speaker) an online event.

Live online programming represents something new and unknown for many librarians and conference organizers. Because it is new and unknown, it often causes us to give free reign to our imaginations. This can be both a blessing and a curse. Without direct, immediate experiential knowledge, many of us tend to amplify both the positive prospects and the potential pitfalls. Often our reaction is to cling to the tried, true, and known forms of group interaction—in this instance, the in-person conference.

Early in February 2006 I had the opportunity to participate in a conference call (how I wish in retrospect it had been a live online meeting!) of a dozen or so librarians who were trying to save an annual in-person conference from a rocky transition phase and possible extinction. The conference had started in the 1990s in response to and as a way to advance an online service movement that had recently emerged in the field of librarianship. This movement had matured to the point that there were established leaders in this sub-field, and most of them were participating in this call.

The conference was at a difficult phase in its existence. The funding and sponsoring organizations that had helped the conference get started and grow had announced that they were no longer able to sponsor and support the conference. The conference had generally broken even in terms of covering its obvious costs, but it was by no stretch of the imagination a cash cow. The folks participating in the conference call just wanted to keep it going.

As the conference call progressed, several basic options were articulated. The conference could continue to be held in a downtown hotel in a medium to large U.S. city, or it could be held on a campus of the college or university, or it could become a combo in-person and online event, or it could become an exclusively online event. The amazing thing about this conference call conversation was the clear preference for the majority of the participants to stick with the first option. Even though the topic of the conference was an online public service component of librarianship, the leading lights of the movement perceived more value in a traditional in-person conference. Several stated that the informal, in-person interactions at previous conferences were greatly valued by the attendees (including the international attendees). Although an online conference or a combo conference could cut costs and extend the opportunity to participate in the conference to other librarians active in this sub-field, the clear preference was to continue a small, rather exclusive in-person conference.

Farkas (2007) provides a good, brief summary of the learning opportunities of online conferences. Farkas emphasizes how online conferences, workshops, and continuing education opportunities can be a cost- and time-efficient complement for in-person events. "For those who receive little support from their institution for continuing education, these [online conferencing and workshop] resources may be just what you need to keep up with the profession." Farkas also stresses the opportunities for members of the virtual studio audience to interact with the speakers or panelists.

COMBO EVENTS

At least two types of combination events are possible. In the first and more common type of combination event, some people are gathered together in person for the event. At the same time, the same event is being distributed to and experienced by others in an online environment.

This type of combo event can be difficult to successfully accomplish on both fronts. Designate one person to serve as the bridge between what's happening in person and what's happening online. The difficulty lies in the fact that an in-person event is experienced differently than a live online event. The environmental stimuli are different, and, more importantly, the pacing is often different.

A second type of combo event attempts to combine a live online group experience with an individualized, self-paced, asynchronous experience. For example, in early 2006 LibraryU Live! and OPAL collaborated to develop a series of asynchronous, self-paced learning modules and live online synchronous components. The live online events often served to introduce a topic, while the hands-on, self-paced learning modules provided more details and experiential knowledge. The two types of online experiences were designed to complement each other.

Many combo events are born out of economic and sociological necessity. Some traditional in-person conferences and other gatherings have witnessed declining interest and attendance in recent years. The conference organizers have been forced to experiment with offering online alternatives. Some in-person conferences may eventually evolve into exclusively online conferences. During the transition phase they may be offered as both in-person and online conferences, eventually jettisoning the in-person part. Or the conference may just switch cold turkey.

HELP THE USER DISCOVER ALL ONLINE EVENTS OF INTEREST

Another way to think beyond the one-shot, one-hour online program is to consider the user's need to discover all upcoming online programs of interest to him or her. The general idea here is that the source of the online program should not impede substantially the ability to discover and access the program. Some sort of online union calendar of upcoming online events—and archived events—would be useful.

FROM ONLINE EVENTS TO ONLINE COMMUNITIES

An online program service can be a goal in itself, or it can be a building block or catalyst for some other larger goal. An ongoing series of quality online programs can be an end in itself, or it could be used to build an online community. Some libraries and library-related organizations see online events as just a means to the bigger goal of creating and sustaining online communities of information seekers and users.

The notion of building and sustaining online communities is very near and dear to several online programming initiatives, including LearningTimes and LibraryU Live! Vibrant online communities have been a goal for various organizations and initiatives for decades.

An online community could be defined as a cohesive group of individuals who share an interest or goal and who communicate with some frequency. In a community the individuals interact in myriad ways, learning about and from each other as they share their similarities and differences. Communities can be notoriously delicate and complex things to incubate and sustain. A community often seems to be the serendipitous outcome of the pursuit of other goals—information, gold, whatever.

CONCLUSION

There are many ways to expand an online program service beyond being just a cluster of largely unrelated, one-time, one-hour online events. As online public programming initiatives proliferate, we probably will witness the refinement of these techniques as the various services strive to attain a niche and differentiate themselves from other online services.

8

Recording, Archiving, and Podcasting Options

CHAPTER SUMMARY

Although the "live" nature of online library programming generates much patron interest and energy during the event, the value of capturing and archiving online events extends the value. Many patrons access an archived online event either because they could not attend the live online event, or because they did not learn about the event until after it had occurred as a live event. When planning online events, consider the "online space" in which the event will occur not only as an auditorium in which the virtual studio audience will assemble virtually for a live online event, but also as a recording studio in which the live online event will be recorded and archived for later distribution and use. Recording, archiving, and redistributing the program content through various means and channels, including podcasting, is an effective and efficient way to increase the impact and usefulness of your online programming efforts. In this chapter you will explore the processes that make this facet of your online library programming initiative both possible and successful.

INTRODUCTION

Web conferencing software can make it very easy to record live online events. Nearly all of the communication in various modes (text chatting, voice-over-IP, and streaming video) as well as the sharing of information (through co-browsing and application sharing) can be recorded. Recording and archiving programs also extends the reach and impact of online library programming. Offering live online library programs allows users to place-shift. They can participate from any Internet-connected spot around the globe. Recording and archiving live online events allows users to time-shift the program to fit their hectic schedules. Both place-shifting and time-shifting make online programs more accessible and useful to more people.

The archives are a vital component of any online program initiative because time-shifting has become a necessity, not just a luxury, for many members of your potential audience. Not everyone can attend a live online program live, even if the fact that it is online means that space-shifting has been essentially solved. In other words, even though the time, effort, and energy it takes to "lug the guts" (as Hamlet said of Polonius) to the site has been overcome through live online programming, the need of many potential users to time-shift must be met, too. Archiving online programs helps solve this problem.

The relationship between the popularity of a live online event and the popularity of a recorded event is neither entirely predictable nor entirely unpredictable. Some online events that don't do well in terms of attracting a sizable virtual studio audience often do surprisingly well as an archived event. Conversely, some online events that draw relatively large numbers to the live online event do not receive much use through the archive.

The components of the archive of recorded live online programs need to be formatted, tagged, and structured so that they are easy to find, understand, and use. Different users of the archive will have different needs, goals, and preferences in using it. Some people will be interested in downloading the audio portion of the recording onto their portable MP3 players. Others may want to quickly slip through the presentation slides to see if listening to and viewing the entire recording will be worth their time. The archival impulse that lurks in all of us to a greater or lesser degree must be assuaged, too. Amazingly, people often ask how to print (gasp) the presentation slides made during a live online event. Usually participants can right click on the slides and choose to print them. Some Web conferencing software makes it easier and fancier to print the slides. Microsoft Office Live Meeting enables participants to print to a PDF file. Creating and maintaining an archive of recorded online programs presents an entirely new set of challenges, but remember that the service opportunities here are great as well.

WHAT CAN BE CAPTURED AND ARCHIVED?

Different Web conferencing software systems offer different functionality and different ways to record what happens during an online event. As the manager of an online programming initiative, look for a recording component within the overall Web conferencing system that enables easy and flexible recording features. Because the primary reason for recording a live online event is usually to share it, look for a system that makes sharing the archived events easy and sustainable. For example, some Web conferencing systems use relatively common file formats for the recording feature, while others use relatively uncommon, often proprietary formats. Some companies that offer hosted Web conferencing services essentially control most aspects of the recording and archiving activities. In essence, you as the coordinator of library programming are merely a customer and consumer of the recording and archiving services the company offers. Other companies allow you to create and manipulate your own recording and archiving. The trade-offs in time and professional recordings may be well worth the effort.

Another key aspect of recording a live online event is the need to aggregate and disaggregate the components of the recording at will to meet various needs. Some downstream users of a recorded live online event will likely want and need to experience the "full recording" of the event, which may include the audio, video, text chat, co-browsing, and other components of the live online event as experienced by the virtual studio audience. These users of the archive really want to experience as fully as possible the online event as it occurred and unfolded. Perhaps even the gaffs and glitches will be of interest and use to some of the "gestalt" users of recorded and archived programs.

Other downstream users may be satisfied with—or even strongly prefer— just one or a few of the components of the full event. The classic example of the need for only a single channel of the recording is the user population for podcasts. At least during the early years of podcasting, the majority of this population of users has expressed a strong preference for receiving the MP3 audio recording of live online events as a segmented, easily distributed, easily transferable, and easily playable component.

The recording and supporting documents for a live online session can be broken into their constituent parts when placed in the archive. For example, an archived event in the OPAL archive may contain:

- the streaming full playback, including audio, text chatting, and any presentation slides or Web pages co-browsed to.
- the audio recording in MP3 file format.
- the presentation slides.
- the text chat log as a separate file.
- any background documents or "handouts" made available during the live online event.

In general, the ability to divide a recording into its constituent parts leads to greater flexibility, usability, and impact of the recorded event. You could podcast the MP3 audio recording, use the text chat file as the rough draft of a set of meeting notes or minutes, download a set of takeaway documents, and so on. If you plan to re-purpose and re-channel the various parts of your recording, some thought must be given to this at the moment of recording. If, for example, a speaker or presenter reads a question or comment in the text chat, then begins responding via VoIP without repeating or summarizing the text chat question or comment, this may cause some confusion to listeners of only the audio recording portion of the archive. Or, conversely, if a speaker mentions a URL during his or her comments, as the event facilitator you may want to type the URL into the text chat box so that when downstream users view and listen to the full playback of the recording, they will see the URL as well as hear it spoken.

Let's briefly review some of the common components of a recorded online live event.

Audio

The audio portion of a live online event is one of the more important and versatile components. MP3 currently is the preferred file format for sharable audio files. However, if the Web conferencing service you use records in another file format, and if the file format is relatively open and convertible, such as the WMA (Windows media audio) file format, there are many no-cost and low-cost software programs available that will allow you to convert the audio file to MP3. Audacity, the free, open-source software program for creating and editing audio files, has plug-ins that enable users to export audio files as MP3, WAV, and ogg vorbis file types.

Ideally, your audio recording of the live event should have no need for editing. If you do see the need to edit an audio file, no-cost and low-cost software is available, such as Audacity, to quickly perform some basic editing of the audio file.

After the audio file is created, you may want or need to revise or add metadata to the file before you make it available to the general public. Because the default metadata fields for audio files assume that the recording is a musical performance, you will want to develop a consistent way of "translating" those default fields to convey information about your spoken word audio recordings. Thus the artist field is used to indicate the speaker, the track field is used for the title of the presentation, and the album field could be used for the name of your online program or your library.

Video

If the Web conferencing service you are using offers video-over-IP, it may be possible to record the video portion of the live online event. Some video recordings are essentially screencasts. Like Camtasia and Jing, these recordings can capture everything happening on your screen. Other video recordings capture just what comes into the Web conferencing room via webcams, such as an image of the speaker or the panel of experts. Recording and delivering high-quality video may require more expertise and bandwidth than the other facets of recording outlined in this chapter. Screen recordings can be good for very screen-intensive demonstrations, where seeing what's happening on the screen is essential to understanding a process. Recordings of webcam images can be useful when you want the downstream users to be able to see the visage of the speaker.

Text Chat

In many Web conferencing systems people can communicate via both voice and text chatting. Text chatting can be either public text chat (where everyone in the online room can see the text chat) or private (where only two or a small group of people in the online room can communicate). Often during the recording of an online event the public text chat is part of the overall recording. In some Web conferencing services, the public text chat also can be saved separately as a simple text file. If the online event contains a lot of text chatting, or if substantive information (such as URLs) are shared via text chat, you may want to consider saving and presenting the text chat as a separate file in your archive.

Attendance

Some Web conferencing systems and services provide a summary account of how many people attended a live online event. One word of caution: often what gets counted is the number of computers (actually, IP addresses) that connected to the Web conferencing server during the time frame of the live online event. If two or more people at any given location are participating in the live online event, the attendance monitoring software may count that as only one participant.

Presentation Slides

There often are various options for presenting slides in a Web conferencing online environment. First, the presentation slides can be saved as HTML pages and uploaded to some server. Then, when the presenter is presenting in a Web conferencing online room, he or she merely co-browses the group to the slide set. Second, in some Web conferencing systems you can load and prsent a set of slides from within the system itself. tcConference from Talking Communities offers a Document Center where PowerPoint slides, Microsoft Word documents, Excel spreadsheets, PDF files, images, and other documents may be uploaded and presented. Third, you may want or need to upload presentation slides into an online whiteboard display, allowing the presenter and/or the participants to doodle on or otherwise mark the slides. Last, you may want to share and modify (individually or as a group) a set of presentation slides using the native software interface, available in the Web conferencing environment through application sharing.

The recording features of the software you are using may handle these different ways of presenting slides in different ways. In fact, some presentation methods may not be included in the recording at all, so proceed with caution. If possible, and if the creator of the presentation slides grants permission, I like to provide a link in an archive just to the presentation slides, because many visitors like to flip through the slides to obtain a sense of the content presented during this online event. The Web server logs for the OPAL archive confirm the fact that many people like to view the slides only.

Handouts, Guides, Webliographies, and More

If an online presentation includes some sort of handout, guide, webliography, or other document, often the best way to include these documents in the recording is to convert them to HTML, upload them to a Web server, then co-browse to them during the live online event being recorded. If the presenter is willing to share the documents in modifiable form with the attendees, make the documents in their native file formats available for downloading from the archive, too.

FILE FORMATS

When it comes to recording, podcasting, and archiving live online programs, pay careful attention to file formats and other technical matters. Each file format has attractive and unattractive aspects and limitations for what you are trying to achieve through your recording, podcasting, and archiving activities.

Since audio and video files tend to be quite large, you will need lots of server space for the archive. The good news here is that the cost of server space continues to decline. Many Web hosting services routinely increase the amount of space allotted to their clients without any cost increase. For example, a one-hour audio recording in WMA format tends to be approximately 9 MB large, and the corresponding MP3 version is about 18 MB large, when converted at a bit rate of 48 Kbps.

POST RECORDING EDITING

Once you have planned, produced, and recorded a live online event, what you are left with, besides the happy memories, is the recording, which is usually one or more rather large files. As the manager of an online library programming initiative, the question becomes, What am I going to do with these files? The recording may be highly polished, with an elegant beginning, middle, and end. Or it may be a little rough around the edges. You can decide to make it available for use as is, or you may want to engage in some form of post-recording editing and manipulation, either to improve the overall quality of the recording or to make it more useful and usable to downstream users.

Post-recording editing and manipulation of these files can take many forms. One option is to upload the files to a server that serves as a light archive where people can access and download the recording. You can also convert one or more components of the recording into other file formats, either to improve the long-term archivability of the recording or to improve its usability. Or you may choose to transfer the recording to various alternative optical and magnetic media, again either primarily to achieve archiving goals or for improved or expanded usability.

PODCASTING

Podcasting, the process of making audio recordings and/or video recordings available online through some syndicated distribution method to which users may subscribe, became very popular in 2005. It has now become so popular and useful that it deserves special mention in the content of recording and archiving live online library programs. Podcasting can be a useful tool for raising awareness and usage of both upcoming and archived online programs.

MP3 files seem to be the preferred file type for podcasting audio recordings, even though most portable MP3 players will also play back WMA and other audio file types, such as Ogg Vorbis.

When converting an audio recording of an online event for podcasting, make sure the bitrate, expressed in kilobits per second, and the frequency response rate, expressed in hertz, that you choose for the output from the conversion fall within the playable ranges for most MP3 players. For example, the frequency response range for the iPod Nano is 20 to 20,000 Hertz (which, coincidentally, is the normal human response rate), and the usable bitrate range for most of the audio file formats supported by the Nano is 16 to 320 kilobits per second (www.apple.com/ipodnano/specs.html).

PROVIDING INTELLECTUAL ACCESS TO THE ARCHIVE

Once you have successfully recorded, podcast, and archived one live online event, you may feel a surge of empowerment. But by the time you have done this for dozens or hundreds of online events, you may feel inundated and overwhelmed with files and data. Organizing and managing this deluge of material can be a big challenge. If you are involved in an online library programming initiative, it's important that you provide an index to the programs in your archive. This helps visitors to the archive find a program even if they remember only the date, the presenter, the organizing library, or the topic. Items in an archive can be placed into the same categories they were put in when they were upcoming programs. Remember, one of the glories of digital information is that you do not need to mark and park each recording only in one place. You can place links to that recording in several places within your index to the archive. Links to a recording of an online presentation about the history of baseball can be placed in both the history and the sports areas of the archive, for example.

Another way to achieve access to the archive is to point a search engine specifically at the archive. As the manager of the Web site supporting the online programming service, you may want to use one of the free Web site indexing and searching services available from Google and other search services. That way, if a user remembers only the topic, presenter, or sponsoring library of an event buried in the archive, he or she should be able to find it quickly through a simple keyword search. In her May 2008 online program about online marketing strategies and tools for libraries, Sarah Houghton-Jan suggests that you could create an iGoogle Gadget that would make it very easy to embed a search box for your library's catalog or archive of recorded programs to any Web page.

Organizing the archived programs can be a challenge. Specifically, coming up with a classification scheme that is sufficiently granular, user-friendly, and also expandable to accurately classify the types of online programs you have offered is difficult. Common sense and flexibility work well in this regard.

PROMOTING AND MEASURING USAGE OF THE ARCHIVE

Web site usage statistics are one way to monitor the usage and impact of recordings you add to the archive of your online programming service. The usage of individual archive files can be impressive, and generally within a few weeks or months after a live online event the archived content receives more usage than there were actual members of the live studio audience.

For example, on December 14, 2005, the Library of Congress conducted a fun and lighthearted OPAL online event called "A Celebration of the Season in Song." Eighteen people attended this live online event. To be correct, eighteen computers connected to the room during this one-hour online program. More than 18 people may actually have been within earshot of those 18 computers. Within an hour after the conclusion of the live online event, the recordings had been put in the archive and podcast. By noon on December 20, less than a week after the online event, the MP3 recording had been accessed 129 times. So, as stated before, these live online events are fun and exciting, but they also are "recording sessions" that are going to reach many more listeners through the archive.

Do archived programs that attracted larger numbers of people to the live online event also receive lots of use? Consider this example. On December 8, 2005, the OPAL collaborative held a live online introduction to podcasting for librarians and information professionals. Ninety-two people were in the virtual studio audience. The MP3 audio recording of the online event was placed in the archive on December 9, 2005. Within ten days the MP3 file had been downloaded 236 times.

How does the usage of an item placed in an archive of programs rise and fall over time? On Wednesday, October 12, 2005, the Library of Congress held a live online event about American inventors and their inventions. Only six people were in the virtual studio audience. Four files related to this event were added to the OPAL archive: the audio recording in both MP3 and WMA file formats, an HTML file that recreates the entire online event (streaming audio, text chat, and co-browsing activity), and a resource guide created by the Library of Congress. The four files were added to the OPAL archive within a couple of hours after the conclusion of the live online event. A podcast announcement also was made about the availability of the MP3 version of the audio recording.

By midnight on Saturday of that week the MP3 file had been downloaded 13 times, the guide 6 times, and the WMA file 2 times. During the following week (October 17–23, 2005), the MP3 file was downloaded 12 times and the guide 2 times. During the next week (October 24–30, 2005), the MP3 file was downloaded 15 times. During the first week in November (October 31 through November 6, 2005), the MP3 file was downloaded 15 times and the guide 2 times. During the second week of November 2005, the MP3 file was downloaded 15 times, the WMA file was downloaded 3 times, and the HTML "full-session" recording 2 times. During the third week of November the MP3 file was downloaded 7 times and the guide 3 times.

This is just one instance of the use of an archived program, but the noticeable points here are that the MP3 audio recording clearly receives the most use, and the usage is fairly steady during the first few weeks immediately following an event. The WMA audio recording, the full-session streaming replay, and the guide received much less—and sporadic—use.

THE CARE AND FEEDING OF AN ARCHIVE

Another policy question concerning a recorded program archive is how long the recorded programs should be kept in the accessible archive. In the best of all possible worlds, all recorded programs would perhaps stay in the archive in perpetuity. However, because these program recordings can be quite large, eventually the amount of storage space required for the recorded programs becomes substantial. Even though the cost of data storage seems to be approaching absolute zero at a steady pace, managing a multiple terabyte archive for one lowly online programming service may become a major headache over time. Secondly, although it is too soon to tell, because online programming services are still relatively new, eventually the demand for certain archived programs may drop to zero and stay there. Eventually you may want to include a "weeding" policy that states, for example, if the Web server logs indicate that the archived files of a recorded program have received no use for two years, they will be removed from the active, open archive and placed in some sort of dark archive.

CONCLUSION

Although the value of the live aspect of live online programs should not be underestimated, the value and impact of archived recordings of live online programs can be substantial. Ranganathan's admonition to save the time of the reader is applicable to a live online programming service, too. An archive of previously recorded live online events allows people to experience them at the places and times that work best for them. While Web conferencing alone allows people to place-shift, an archive of recorded online events allows people to place-shift and time-shift.

9

Evaluating an Online Programming Service

CHAPTER SUMMARY

Once you've launched your online programming service, you may wonder how effective it is, or you may be asked to report on its effectiveness to your superiors. In this chapter you will explore ways to assess and evaluate your online programming service. There are many possible reasons for undertaking an evaluation of an online programming service, and there are many possible stakeholders in such an evaluation process. For example, an evaluation undertaken primarily for an external funding agency that supports the online programming service may be different in form, scope, and content than an evaluation undertaken as a professional research and publication initiative.

Many sources of data, information, and opinion can inform your evaluation process. Formal and informal user feedback, usage data, and other types of data can help inform the process.

Libraries, library professionals, and members of the general public who participate as members of the virtual studio audience in live online events will also want to perform some type of assessment and evaluation of the online events they attend, even if only to answer the basic question, "Was attending this live event worthwhile?"

Whereas impact and quality programming may be key outcomes desired by the designers and providers of online programming, for those who attend live online events a main evaluation criterion may be cost avoidance. In other words, is the live, online method of providing continuing education for the public, and for staff and professional development, sufficiently rich, robust, and sticky (meaning, Do the knowledge and skills learned online stick with you?) to justify not incurring the substantially higher cost of attending the same or similar event in person? Although the answer to that question will vary from individual to individual and from institution to institution, for many members of a virtual studio audience, avoiding the costs of time and travel to an in-person event can be a major factor in assessing the value and impact of a live online event.

INTRODUCTION

Obtaining useful feedback from attendees about an online public program can be challenging. Be sure to gather feedback both from attendees of your live online programs as well as from users of your archived programs and podcasts.

One of the best and most obvious ways to assess user needs is to ask people about their needs and preferences regarding online programming. Of course, some people—perhaps all of us—have a difficult time sensing or articulating a need until some service is presented that addresses the heretofore unrecognized need. Because this seems to be a basic human characteristic, you may want to examine community profiles and census data to get a general sense of the potential audience for your service, at least locally. Nevertheless, anecdotal feedback from individual users of your service can be useful. It also is possible to assess user needs and desires regarding future online programs in the midst of a current online program. Sometimes during an OPAL program—usually near the end—we ask people to provide immediate feedback and ideas for future programs. They can do this via private or public text chat within an OPAL room.

It also is possible to push a formal feedback survey out to the members of a virtual studio audience, usually near the end of an event.

EVALUATING THE SOFTWARE AND SYSTEM

At least one, and perhaps a number of the questions to address in your evaluation is how well your program software and system have supported your online program. Did the voice-over-IP function work well for everyone who used it? Was the presenter able to co-browse everyone to the Web sites he or she wanted to show and discuss? Did the recording function of the software perform as advertised?

When using a hosted Web conferencing service, absolute downtime—when the system simply is unavailable—is rare. Much more common are minor problems that can be placed under the general rubric of server glitches. The potential causes of these glitches are numerous: heavy Internet traffic, operator error by the moderator or speaker, problems at the recipient's end, solar flares, or actually brief server malfunctions. What typically happens is that one or more persons in the virtual studio audience get temporarily kicked off the server and thus removed from the online meeting room. Although they usually pop right back in, this can be annoying to individuals and the entire group.

EVALUATING PROGRAM FORMATS

Remember also to evaluate the various program formats, such as the lecture format by a single presenter, a roundtable or panel discussion, an interview, a demonstration, a virtual tour, and an "open mic" discussion. In a feedback survey to attendees you may want to inquire about the pacing and flow of the online event. People's tolerance for short periods of silence may be lower online than at an in-person event, or the lag time between when a presenter begins talking about a presentation slide and when the slide actually appears on an attendee's computer monitor may be sufficiently annoying to prompt that attendee to give the online event an overall low rating. Any type of rapid give-and-take conversation between an interviewer and an interviewee, or between members of a panel discussion, can be difficult to accomplish via Web conferencing software. As with other media, some program formats work better than other program formats.

EVALUATING PROGRAMS BY CONTENT CATEGORIES

How useful or interesting are the topics of your online programs? One way to gauge interest is by number of registrants. Even though other factors (such as the time of the program or how well it was publicized) affect live online participation, programs that draw the highest number are probably some of the more interesting. Another measure is the number of times the recordings have been accessed. Of course, ratings and comments by participants should be used as well. Recently, two author interviews were held in OPAL. One author had written an award-winning novel for young adults. The other author had written a book about marketing strategies for libraries. Both books had been published just a few months before the online author interviews. Interestingly, the online interview with the author of the library marketing book drew ten times the number of live online participants than did the online interview with the author of the award-winning young adult novel. What conclusions should we draw from this fact? In general, online programs on topics of interest to librarians tend to attract more attendees than online programs on topics of interest to the general public. Perhaps the service needs to try different methods of making the public aware of the free, online programs offered. Perhaps the current economic downturn has redoubled the interest and efforts of libraries to reach out effectively to the communities they serve.

EVALUATING THE INDIVIDUAL PROGRAMS

Each online program seems to have its own unique personality, influenced by the personality and preparedness of the presenter, the makeup and general mood of the live studio audience, the topic, the technology, the time of the day, the day of the week, the month of the year, and so on. Sometimes the members of the live online audience will use the text chat feature extensively to comment on what the presenter is saying or to chat and joke with each other. Other times they will sit on their hands and just listen. It is often difficult to predict which basic personality type an upcoming online program will manifest.

Most Web conferencing systems provide means for members of the virtual studio audience to give immediate feedback to the presenter. A member of the virtual studio audience can always type something such as "absolutely" or "right on" or "what a load of crap" into the text chat box in response to what the speaker is saying at the time. The Elluminate software allows people to clap or give a thumbs up or down sign spontaneously or when prompted by the speaker, presenter, or facilitator. The tcConference Web conferencing software from Talking Communities offers participants a palette of emoticons to choose from to expresses their mood or reaction to what is being said. The old saying at in-person conferences was that participants vote with their feet. In other words, if you find yourself in a conference session that is poorly presented, deadening to your cranium, falsely advertised, or just not of interest to you, get up and leave. In online events, the principle is the same, but you vote with a mouse click, not with your feet. One interesting phenomenon is that people often do not leave the room once an online event begins. If they do need to leave, they often apologize that they need to leave to go attend a live in-person meeting. Many people may simply tune out—that is, turn their attention elsewhere—without actually leaving the online room.

Remember, online room statistics usually record the number of computers —not people—that connect to the room. The SirsiDynix Institute in its feedback survey asks specifically how many people were huddled around the computer that was connected to the online meeting room. It also asks for suggested topics for future online seminars.

Another way to evaluate individual online programs is to assess *who* attended. Online programming may reach a different segment of the public and/or the library profession than typically attends live in-person events.

The online program, then, can be assessed in terms of its ability to reach a heretofore segment of the service population that was difficult or impossible to reach.

In 2006, the OPAL collaborative offered an online program on the topic of sustaining small rural libraries. The program was well attended by librarians from various geographic locations, many of them far from urban areas, such as western Kansas and northern Maine. Several attendees to this live online event commented on the fact that they would have been unable to attend a similar in-person event, even if it had been held in their own state, because they could not afford the travel costs, travel time, and loss of manpower at that small library.

EVALUATING THE PRESENTERS

Collecting evaluation information about individual presenters can be a touchy issue. Many presenters of online programs are doing this for the first time—or have been doing it for just a short while—so they may not yet feel accustomed to and comfortable with the Web conferencing mode of delivering a presentation or conducting a workshop or training session. In addition, many presenters observe that receiving little or no nonverbal cues from the live virtual audience can be unnerving, or that seeing text chat comments from participants disrupts their own thought processes and presentation style. It can be difficult to maintain a perky mien for 60 minutes when you receive such little reinforcement and feedback from your audience. However, evaluating the presenter's performance is imperative to the review process.

Why? First of all, because presenters generally want to know how they did and how they can improve the effectiveness and style of future online events they may lead or facilitate. In addition, the success of your programs relies in part on the presenter's abilities and skills, so you must solicit feedback on or otherwise rate the presenter.

As the program coordinator who has witnessed many different online presenters, you will likely want to provide some pointers before an individual presenter presents, and some informal feedback after that presenter has presented. A key goal in this regard is to make the presenter comfortable with and confident in the Web conferencing technology being used so that he or she can concentrate on the presentation, not on the technology being used.

LEARNING MORE ABOUT THE DEMOGRAPHICS, NEEDS, PREFERENCES, AND REACTIONS OF ATTENDEES

For certain types of online public programs the library or consortium may want to collect certain contact information (such as email addresses) and basic demographic information (the state or nation in which the participants live, their sexes, and ages) from attendees. Of course, requiring potential attendees to register beforehand is one venue for obtaining that information. Another way is to gather that information just before they enter the online meeting room.

This type of information even can be collected once the virtual studio audience is seated in the online room, by conducting a poll or asking members of the virtual studio audience to type in their location and institutional affiliation. Bear in mind, however, that some members of the virtual studio audience may opt out of this type of self-disclosure; and it is even conceivable that some members of the virtual studio audience may choose to dissemble and report false information. Collecting demographic information via in-room text chatting also can require a considerable amount of time and effort, especially if it requires you to go back through the text chat transcript and pull the self-reported information into a more concise and usable form.

To gather ideas for future online programs, ask members of the virtual studio audience to share their ideas near the end of an online program, especially if the online program has been particularly good and energizing. If the program is about a technology topic, you could ask people to suggest other tech topics of interest to them. If the program is a book discussion, you could ask the group for titles, authors, or genres they would like to discuss online in the future.

Some members of the virtual studio audience may have no qualms or reluctance about sharing their ideas in public text chat. If, however, private text chatting is available in the Web conferencing service you are using for your online programming initiative, you can also encourage members of the virtual studio audience to share their ideas and opinions with you via private text chat. Be sure to remind them that their feedback will remain anonymous and confidential. You could also type your email address into the public text chat area and encourage members of the virtual studio audience to email you after the current online event has concluded.

EVALUATING THE USE AND USEFULNESS OF THE ARCHIVE

If, as the manager of an online programming service, you find that recorded and archive programs consistently receive more use than the live online programs, this presents a special evaluation challenge. It is easier to bring to the attention of members of the virtual studio audience at the live event the availability and value of a feedback process than to users of the archived content. Users of your archive of previous, recorded live online events may remain well-nigh inscrutable to you. Generally, all you can do is watch what gets clicked on and used.

Server logs provide good data for the purposes of assessing a Web archive of previous, recorded live online events, but they do have limitations. Server logs only measure the fact that people loaded a Web page, started streaming some audio, or downloaded a file. They cannot really tell you for certain that the person who loaded a Web page actually read it, or that the person who started streaming some audio content actually listened to the entire recording, or that someone who downloaded a file eventually opened it, perhaps after transferring it to another device, such as an MP3 player.

In this regard, server logs are similar to circulation statistics of the "use" of a collection of printed books. Circulation statistics confirm that a patron checked out a book (and presumably took the copy out of the library), but what that patron did with the book from that point until returning it remains a mystery. The patron may have read part of the book, then left off for some reason. Or the patron may have read the entire book—twice or three times. Or perhaps the user used that heavy tome merely to press some flowers. We cannot say for certain. In the same manner, we cannot know for certain exactly what people do when they load a Web page, start streaming some content, or begin downloading a file.

If you podcast audio recordings of previous live online events, the podcasting service you use may provide you with some usage statistics. If your library or library-related organization uses some tangible distribution method, such as CDs or flash memory cards, as a method of distributing archived online programs, you can easily tabulate the popularity and costs of this component of your archive service.

EVALUATING YOUR ANNOUNCEMENT AND PROMOTIONAL EFFORTS

The old adage among advertisers is, "We know 50 percent of what we do is a waste of time and money; we're just not sure which 50 percent is the waste." The same adage could apply to the methods you use to announce and promote your online programming initiative, both as an initiative and for the individual upcoming programs.

One simple way to reveal the invisible tendrils of your announcing and promotional efforts is to simply ask the members of a virtual studio audience to type into text chat how they heard about the program they are attending. Sometimes they will mention some communication channel that you initiated, such as the monthly YouTube video announcements that I do for upcoming OPAL online programs. Other times they will mention some communication channel that was not initiated by you but represents the fact that electronic communications can be forwarded ad nauseam. I remember vividly when one attendee at an online program reported that he had heard about the event through some electronic communication from the Tulane University Law School.

Most blogging services allow readers to attach comments to a post. If the blog post is an announcement of an upcoming or archived online program, the comments can become part of the overall feedback picture.

EVALUATING THE ENTIRE SERVICE

Ultimately, you must evaluate the entire online programming service . Such an evaluation could concentrate on the cost-benefit ratio of the service. Before doing so, however, you need to have a clear sense of what your organization wants and needs the service to achieve. For some services, having just a few large online events each year that attract hundreds or thousands of users may be a major criterion for measuring the success of the service. Other services, however, may be striving to offer a wide variety of dozens or hundreds of events each year that attract smaller, niche audiences.

Cost avoidance is one way to justify a Web conferencing system for your library, library-related organization, or their parent organizations. If the librarians at your library attend an average of 50 statewide meetings per year, you can monitor or project the expenses that 50 in-person meetings would entail, including staff time actually attending the meeting, drive time, meals, and the cost of transportation. If through the use of Web conferencing software your library can decrease the annual number of in-person attendance at statewide meetings to 25, you can calculate cost avoidance in terms of the transportation costs and drive-time costs of those 25 meetings that have converted from in-person to online meetings.

CONCLUSION

Evaluating an online programming service requires some inventiveness and persistence. By engaging in some ongoing assessment and evaluation activities, you will achieve a better sense of the overall value and success of your service, as well as many ideas for improving the service and for reaching other segments of the population you serve.

10

Key Issues

CHAPTER SUMMARY

This chapter explores several of the "big issues" related to online library programming as a major public programming effort for libraries of all types. The big issues include some of the intractable conditions and opportunities facing online programming services.

INTRODUCTION

Like any library service, online library programming has developed a cluster of issues and points of tension or disagreement. Here we briefly explore some of these key issues.

WHY DON'T LIBRARIES AND LIBRARY-RELATED ORGANIZATIONS USE WEB CONFERENCING SOFTWARE MORE?

In this age of high and rising travel and transportation costs, when multitasking has become the norm, and multichannel communication (voice, text chat, and nonverbal visual information) has come to be expected, why do libraries and library-related organizations seem reluctant to use Web conferencing software more than they currently do?

Ignorance may be part of the answer to this question. Perhaps many librarians simply do not know or are only vaguely aware of the power, flexibility, reliability, affordability, and simplicity of Web conferencing software. Web conferencing software became branded early in its history as something very techie that was designed primarily for well-funded organizations, such as large corporations and military units. Although prices have been dropping as the features continue to grow and improve, the initial impression that Web conferencing systems are really for technologically proficient and well-heeled users is difficult to overcome.

Some libraries and library-related systems invested heavily in closed circuit television systems, which really never completely panned out as an alternative to in-person meetings. Because of this historical situation, many library and library-related organizations may be reluctant to hurriedly invest in and try Web conferencing systems.

Web conferencing systems never had their technological day in the sun, when they were the hot new wave of the future, the darlings of the media, the object of much conversation and speculation, and so on. Compare the fate in the public imagination of Web conferencing with electronic books, which certainly have had their day in the digital sun. Although e-books continue to struggle mightily to find their place in the overall reading habits of the public, the fact that they were once fodder for the hype machine has provided them with a long tail of general interest, if not concomitant use.

One other detail that might be a deterrent to adoption is that the multichannel form of most Web conferencing systems may be off-putting to many librarians. Text chatting while listening to a speaker or some sort of presentation may be perceived by many librarians as distracting for both the speakers and the audience, or simply rude and inconsiderate. And text chatting may be perceived by many librarians as something that young people do as a type of informal and inconsequential communication, but massive text chatting during library-sponsored online public events may be seen by many librarians as "beneath" the library as a public good institution with an august social and cultural mission.

Further, many libraries have such tight budgets that it can be very difficult to find any discretionary funds to invest in the technology that makes Web conferencing-based online programming possible. Plus, the tech support staffs at many libraries already are overworked and are reluctant to provide local implementation support for a Web conferencing system. Nevertheless, interest by libraries, library-related organizations, and individual librarians in the power, ease, and convenience of online programs delivered via Web conferencing continues slowly grow. Time will tell if some tipping point will be reached soon.

MAJOR ARGUMENTS AGAINST ONLINE LIBRARY EVENTS

Several criticisms can be made against the idea of using Web conferencing software to develop and deploy a public online programming service. The first criticism grows from the fact that it is much more difficult to attract public participants to online events than it is to attract librarians and information professionals. The argument goes that rather than squander precious time and energy trying to cajole the public to attend and participate in public online events, perhaps libraries and library-related organizations should focus on using Web conferencing software as an intra-profession tool for hot topic programs, continuing education, training, and professional development.

The problem with jettisoning the public component of online programming is that such an action would fly against the social purpose of most libraries. Libraries ultimately exist to serve the public, or at least some defined subset of the general public, such as the citizens living in the geographic region known as the library district, or the students, faculty, and staff of a school, school district, college, or university. Yes, my experiences with OPAL confirm that it is more difficult to attract the public to online events than librarians, but I assert that we must continue to try to attract the public. If we use Web conferencing software strictly as an inhouse tool for professional and organizational communication, we run the risk of further charges of navel-gazing and further erosion of public support for the future of libraries. Web conferencing is really still in its infancy—its formative years. If we allow it to mature only as a tool for professional communication, it will be difficult to expand its use down the road for public online events. If we extend online programming to our public, it will, over time, build in strength and numbers, all the while building our image as a dynamic profession serving society.

Something similar may have happened to the library catalog, which initially developed as an inventory control system for use by librarians and library staff to keep track of and describe the items contained in the collection. Much of the current criticism being leveled at online public access catalogs centers on the fact that they never really integrated the public access component into the very fabric of catalog design.

Another major criticism of online public programming turns one of the undeniable strengths of this technology on its head. Web conferencing software allows people to get together, communicate, share ideas, and work collaboratively without requiring the burning of vast quantities of fossil fuels. In other words, it allows people to meet without traveling to a common location. If a library offers a slate of online programs that are open to everyone, regardless of their geographic location, the programs may (and probably will) attract people who are not members of the core population to be served by the library presenting the program.

This criticism of public online programming gets at one of the fundamental problems of current and future librarianship. In an era when the seeking and use of information by individuals and work groups is global, most libraries tend to rely heavily on geographically limited funding schemes. And most libraries have a geographically constrained definition of their core service population. Although very few libraries can legitimately claim the world's population as their core service population, online public programming move libraries closer to the vision of making their services available to anyone who wants or needs to use those services.

In response to this criticism, it may be useful to point out that, in the best of all possible worlds, and in the light of current trends in networked access to digital information and communication resources, it appears that the current definitions of the core service populations of most libraries is the problem, not the global accessibility of online public programming through the use of Web conferencing software.

ONLINE VERSUS IN-PERSON

One common and frequently recurring fear about any technology is that it will not only disrupt the status quo but also absolutely replace technologies, social structures, and cultural graces we know and love. Electronic books were predicted by some to kill paper books, just as in earlier eras television was predicted to kill radio, the horseless carriage was going to kill the horse (or at least put them all out to pasture), and the VCR was going to kill the movie theater business. What usually happens when a new technology appears is that the new technology somewhat diminishes the popularity of the existing technology, but ultimately it tends to be additive more than subtractive. For example, in the late nineteenth century the horse population in the United States was estimated to be approximately 8 million. In 1999, almost a century after the introduction of the automobile, the horse population stood at 5.3 million (http://usda.mannlib.cornell.edu/reports/nassr/livestock/equine/equi1999.txt). So it should not come as a surprise that the idea has surfaced that online programming (events, workshops, conferences) will kill in-person events of the same nature.

National library associations, state library associations, and newer library-related organizations, such as LibraryU and WebJunction, are trying to discern the evolving future relationship between online programs and in-person programs. Some library-related organizations have adopted a strategy of offering combination events—both in-person and online. In mid-October 2005 the Wyoming Library Association and the Mountain Plains Library Association held a joint conference that was both a traditional in-person conference—in Jackson Hole, Wyoming, no less—and an online conference as a webcast. The emphasis of this combo event was more on the traditional in-person happenings than on the online happenings.

Although members of the virtual studio audience could listen to and view the conference talks, they could not ask questions or make comments, nor could they tell how many or who else was participating online.

Also in mid-October 2005, the Illinois Library Association held its annual conference in Peoria. As an experiment, the panel discussion on top technology trends was recorded, archived in both WMA and MP3 audio file formats, and a podcast announcement (http://opalpodcast.blogspot.com /2005/10/library-information-technology-trends.html) about the availability of the MP3 file was made. Approximately 100 people attended the live in-person event, which is typical for this type of event at the annual conference of the Illinois Library Association. By the end of the 2005 calendar year, the MP3 recording of this session had been downloaded from the archive 387 times. The WMA recording was a distant second, not even reaching 100 downloads. Through this simple, inexpensive technology of online program archiving and podcasting, the content of this panel discussion held at the annual conference of the Illinois Library Association reached approximately four times as many people as it normally does as an in-person-only event.

Rather than offer combination in-person/online events, other library associations and library-related organizations are alternating between in-person and online events. This method cuts down on annual travel time and expenses without abandoning the value and benefits of in-person interaction.

One wrinkle to the online versus in-person big issue concerns the future of professional conferences and workshops. Conferences often generate income over expenses for the associations that organize them. Online conferences have not yet proven that they can consistently generate the type of revenue that in-person conferences generate, even if the expenses of holding an online conference are lower than the expenses of an in-person conference. Library associations find themselves in a situation similar to those of newspaper companies, publishers, and pornographers (disruptive technologies make for strange bedfellows!): the revenue stream for online events is much murkier and muddier than the known print-based and in-person revenue streams.

The advantages of online events include lower cost and time commitment and the opportunity to sit in your own chair and sleep in your own bed. The disadvantages include the need to supply your own snacks, refreshments, and happy hour libations.

Online events present a wonderful opportunity for the mingling of different groups and social strata. On the Internet, no one knows you're a new librarian. For example, if a live in-person literary event is scheduled to be held on a college or university campus, chances are slim that such an event would draw many participants from the general population. The very fact that it will be held on a campus deters people who are not currently affiliated with an academic institution. They often surmise that the conversation will be too scholarly or that they will somehow not be made to feel welcome. If the same event were held in an online meeting room, however, the campus stigma would not apply. During the online book discussion of Willa Cather's novel *My Antonia*, the participants included college professors, graduate students, librarians, and members of the general public. Everyone had something to say and contribute.

Another advantage of live online events over in-person events is that online programs can provide an outlet to utterances of expertise from the members of the virtual studio audience. We all have experienced the situation at a conference or workshop where one or more members of the audience have at least as much knowledge about the topic as do one or more of the official panelists. Often this situation becomes apparent only during the question and answer period near the end of the live in-person discussion. In online environments, however, often the pockets of expertise within the virtual studio audience make themselves manifest sooner and more easily. One reason this may be so is because there usually are two or more communication channels within an online meeting room that are competing for everyone's attention. The text chat exchanges may complement, contradict, or run parallel to the message coming across via VoIP, for instance. Although something like this occasionally happens during a live in-person event (such as someone sitting next to you leans over and mutters a comment while the speaker is speaking, or one panelist writes on a flip chart while another speaks), the effective use of dual or multiple channels of communication is much less common during in-person events than in live online events.

LIVE VERSUS RECORDED (SYNCHRONOUS VERSUS ASYNCHRONOUS)

There is something eminently attractive and endearing about live events—glitches, warts, and all. Most human beings like the immediacy and undetermined nature of live events. We seem to be willing—at least occasionally—to exchange the polish and predictable consistent quality of prerecorded events, such as motion pictures and musical performances recorded and mixed in recording studios, for the excitement and mystery (What will happen next?) of live events.

Live, in-person events, such as cultural performances (plays, musical concerts) and sporting events (football games and the Olympics), often generate the highest levels of human interest. Live distributed events, such as television and radio broadcasts of cultural and sporting events, generate a high level of interest, too. We expect events that are produced in studios, such as motion pictures, television shows, and music albums, to have a certain level of production polish and quality, regardless of what we think of the polish and quality of the content itself. With live events, part of the attraction is the lack of polish and the sense that anything may happen, especially if Janet Jackson and Justin Timberlake are part of the halftime show.

During a conference call in January 2006, Jonathan Finkelstein from LearningTimes noted that one benefit of large online events—events that attract over 100 participants—is that they are a particularly effective way to launch an online community that engages in a sustained, fruitful discussion about a topic, a problem, or an opportunity. There is a certain energy about these online events that is capable of forming a new community out of a ball of gas and hot air and propelling it forward toward some goal. In the digital universe, live events can wind up the clock. Live in-person events also can achieve the same result. Just think of how many initiatives bear the name of the location at which the core group originally met. Dublin Core is an example.

In-person, live events, however, are much more expensive to hold and attend, thus creating a certain de facto exclusivity about them. Most people interested in a live event, from the smallest poetry reading to the largest mass media extravaganza, cannot afford to attend the live event in person. Because of the logistics involved, in-person live events also require more lead time to plan and pull off than the typical live online event.

Live, in-person events as the catalyst and propellant for a new community of interest or endeavor also face the difficult challenge of how to transition the energy of an in-person, carbon-based nascent community to an online, electron-based effective community. Communities that are energetic and effective in person are not always as effective when operating online, and vice versa.

The very characteristics of live events that make them attractive—the thrill of the unknown, the potential for mistakes and gaffs, and the sense that something experienced live is a real experience—also are the qualities that give their organizers fits. Trying to pull off a successful live event involves the assumption of significant amounts of a wide variety of risks. What if the technology fails? Even live, in-person events rely significantly on technology. For live outdoor events, the weather may prove uncooperative. The performers or presenters involved in a live event may mess up. Members of the audience or the audience as a whole may act up or become unruly.

For mass media outlets, such as radio and television, which began entirely as live programming, the risks of live events were just too great and too unreliable. The history of radio and television over the past 50 years has been marked by the gradual decline in the amount of live programming offered. The morning talk shows now are live only in the Eastern Time Zone, and even then there probably is an intentional delay built into the broadcast, in case of some sort of technology failure or human error. The same is true with "live" sporting events, which now have a fewer minutes of lag time buffered into the broadcasts. Although the meaning of a "live" event continues to evolve as different technologies are used to convey events and information, many program developers and presenters across all media are embracing the idea of have some lag-time built into the system, in case something goes wrong.

Online events that are as live as they can be, given the vagaries of network connections and network traffic, convey to participants the sense that these are "real" events, a sense that online and virtual events desperately need.

PROFESSIONAL DEVELOPMENT PROGRAMS VERSUS PUBLIC PROGRAMS

Library publishers (e.g., *Library Journal*), library vendors (e.g., SirsiDynix), library consortia (e.g., Solinet), and library associations (e.g., the American Library Association) are successfully using Web conferencing software to offer online professional development and current awareness programs for librarians and other information professionals. So far, the practice of "rank and file" libraries offering online programming to the general public seems to be lagging behind.

Based on my experiences and observations since 2008, I admit that online programming tends to be more in demand among librarians and other information professionals than it is among the general public. Although we do not ask librarians to declare their profession when they attend an OPAL online event, the events that have been geared more toward librarians, such as the program on library services for older adults, generally have had larger virtual studio audiences than have programs geared more toward the general public.

This imbalanced situation may change over time as more members of the general public learn about the richness and convenience of online programming services, but it creates an interesting short-term conundrum. Should a library or group of collaborating libraries spend most of their collective time and energy on creating professional development programs for librarians and other information professionals, or should they focus primarily on online public programming? In some ways, this is a zero-sum game. There is only so much time, energy, and expertise that any library or group of libraries can devote to an online programming service.

Of course, for library-related organizations, such as consortia, library systems, library vendors, some publishers, and associations, librarians are the primary service population. It makes perfect sense for them to develop and deliver online programs geared toward their core service population. For the typical public, school, academic, or special library, however, their core service population consists primarily of non-librarians. Online programming services may be accused of offering quite a few professional development and enrichment programs in order to generate high-attendance online events that increase the overall average attendance for the entire corpus of online programs.

This conundrum cannot be resolved simply. If I had a nickel for every in-person library conference program where someone mentioned that they wished more vendors, publishers, authors, information technologists, and members of the general public attended library conference programs, I would have at least a buck. With an online programming service it may be much easier to attract a crossover or mixed virtual studio audience. One reason for this is that people from different fields and socioeconomic backgrounds can attend without fearing that their clothing or the color of their conference badge will declare to all in attendance their affiliations, allegiances, and predilections. One advantage of online programs is that individual members of the live virtual audience can declare as little or as much about themselves as they wish. They even can attend under pseudonyms or via stand-in avatars. Ultimately, the basic constraints and opportunities offered by online environments in this regard are an improvement over the constraints and opportunities presented by an in-person meeting environment, and this eventually will result in better, livelier online events with cross-pollination of ideas and best practices among various professions and social segments.

By early 2006, online programming had proven its value to library-related organizations (library associations, library consortia, state libraries, library vendors, and trade publishers focused on library and information technology professionals). Online events geared toward librarians consistently draw online studio audiences in the upper two-digit and lower three-digit range. The big question is, Will library users eventually become attracted to online public programming being offered by "rank-and-file" libraries? Since the sizes of virtual studio audiences for online events geared toward library users are usually considerably smaller than for professional development events for librarians, should online programming initiatives such as OPAL and LibraryU Live! throw in the towel regarding true public programming and concentrate on professional development programs?

PAY ATTENTION

There is an attention problem with online events that must be noted. The problem has several facets. One part of the problem is that, when in-person events are held, they are usually held in closed rooms, and locations that are fairly austere, where the opportunities of being distracted are minimized. Most convention center rooms, for example, have few or no windows. In contrast, in the foyers and hallways where intermissions are held, there usually are plenty of windows. So, other than observing the other people at the online event, or Twittering, or surfing the Web, there usually is not much to tug at the attention of in-person attendees.

When the online event is held on one's computer, however, the opportunities for distractions multiply. People can browse in their browsers, read their email, and work on documents while participating in an online event. This ability to multitask while attending an online event is a double-edged sword. It can make the attendees more productive, building on the advantage of avoiding the downtime of traveling to an in-person event, but it also can create an attention problem for the virtual studio audience as a whole.

Another facet of this problem is that the environment of the meeting and the real environment in which each attendee lives and breathes are interwoven in time. Real world needs and interruptions, such as bathroom breaks, someone poking his or her head into your cubicle to ask a quick question, ringing phones, barking dogs, fire alarms, and so on, can impinge on the overall effectiveness of an online event. And the organizers of the online event have no control over the dispersed patchwork quilt of real world environmental conditions where their participants are. If the air conditioning or electricity goes out at a convention center, everyone in attendance is affected. If the telephones in the offices of seven out of 100 people attending a live online event ring, the other 93 usually are oblivious to these interruptions, but the effectiveness and success of the overall online event may suffer slightly because of these pixilated distractions.

A third facet of this problem is that the speaker and event organizer cannot gauge the level of attention of the virtual studio audience as a whole. As a speaker, you cannot survey your audience to get a sense of how many are paying attention, becoming restive, getting distracted, or falling asleep.

The speaker or presenter during a live online event faces a double challenge regarding gaining and holding the attention of the virtual studio audience. The first challenge is that, compared to venues of most in-person events, there are many more sources of distractions in a live online event. These sources tend to cluster into three types: in the environs of each participant, in other applications running on their computers, and in other features of the Web conferencing software being used.

People are sitting in front of their computers during live online events, often the same place where they sit day after day completing their work-related tasks. These familiar ambient real-world environs in which the members of your virtual studio audience sit can draw their attention away from the online program. Phones have a nasty habit of ringing at inopportune times, people pop into cubicles, and severe weather events happen frequently. For participants attending from home, dogs may bark, babies may cry, and doorbells may ring. Unlike in-person events, where the organizers and presenters have some control over the ambient local environment shared by all participants, with an online event you have little or no control over these distributed and localized sources of distraction. More than once I have had participants report that a violent thunderstorm is passing over them as they participate in an online event, or there is a fire alarm in the building in which they sit.

The other applications people usually have running on their networked computers while they attend an online event offer another cluster of potential distractions. Because most Web conferencing software systems allow members of the virtual studio audience to minimize the online room window and still be able to hear the discussion occurring in the online room, many may be working on other tasks on their computers while they participate in an online event. It can be very tempting to work on other computer tasks while listening to an online event. Furthermore, many email and instant messaging systems are configured by default to emit a sound announcing the arrival of a new message, which can be distracting to members of your virtual studio audience. The use of Twitter as a "backchannel" for communication among attendees of online events (as well as in-person events) is becoming very popular, with conference hashtags decided and announced before the event begins.

Even within the online meeting room itself, there are many potential sources of distraction. Text chat and private text chat messages can temporarily or permanently draw a participant's attention away from the main message of the online event. Most Web conferencing systems have an embedded browser window, and most systems allow individual members of a virtual studio audience to browse unilaterally at will. Again, this can draw attention away from the speaker and his or her message.

The second attention challenge for the organizers and presenters of an online event is that not only do they have little or no control over potential distractions to the attention of the members of their virtual studio audience, they usually have little or no way of knowing if a large percentage of the members of the virtual studio audience have divided their attentions to other stimuli or tasks.

This situation varies considerably from that of a typical live in-person event. Have you ever noticed that many meeting halls and conference centers are sparsely decorated? In most meeting rooms in hotels and convention centers, the most interesting and potential attention-grabbing feature of the room—other than one's fellow attendees—are the lighting fixtures. The walls, chairs, tables, and floors usually are pretty bland, drab, and uninteresting. Sensory deprivation is one way to try to hold someone's attention.

Most Web conferencing systems offer both subtle and overt means for trying to retain and focus the attention of the members of the virtual studio audience. Unilateral browsing from within the application can be blocked, forcing everyone to view the Web sites and presentation slides being pushed by the presenter. In some systems it also is possible to prohibit private text chatting between two members of the virtual studio audience. Although these features may be enticing, my advice is to avoid using these system "crutches" to gain and retain the attention of the participants. Let the program content or delivery sink or swim on its own merits. If you try to lock down your Web conferencing system so that it cannot be used for informal communication and information seeking, most attendees of the live online event may conclude that Web conferencing events are significantly denuded, compared to live in-person events.

Another aspect of crowd control involves participants who arrive late for an online event, after the program is underway. Usually the entry of a new participant triggers some sort of an alerting system to everyone else in the online room. A message may appear in the text chat transcript area that Susie Q. Public has joined the session. An audible sound (a ding or a chime) may accompany the entry of each new participant. When this occurs prior to the start of the event, it fuels the building excitement for the upcoming event. When it occurs after the online event has begun, it is distracting to the speaker and everyone else in the online room, and it may annoy some who arrived on time.

Late arrivals also present several other practical challenges. Because the flow and rhythm of the online event has been interrupted, the speaker may pause and welcome the new participant, letting him or her know in a sentence where the group is in the progress of the online event. This works well with single-presenter, highly structured presentations, but less well for loosely structured group discussions, musical performances, and other types of programs. If co-browsing is already underway, the newly arrived participant may not be in synch with everyone else in the online room. Depending on the Web conferencing system you are using, that may necessitate having the event coordinator or even the presenter refresh the screen. As you explore Web conferencing systems and software, be sure to examine how each system handles late arrivals.

The flip side of the late arriving crowd is the early departers, who leave the online room before the online event officially ends. Some people who need to leave early will announce their departure and apologize before they zip off ("Sorry, I need to be on the reference desk in five minutes. Great program. Thanks!"). Others will simply exit the room, which again often triggers some sort of visual and auditory signal that someone has left the online event.

For those who leave abruptly, the presenter, the event organizer, and the other members of the virtual studio audience have no idea why that person left. He or she may have been bumped off the server. When that happens, the person often pops back into the room within a few seconds. If the person doesn't come back, it leaves everyone wondering—however fleetingly—what happened. Perhaps they couldn't stand the online event. Perhaps some offline emergency forced them to leave abruptly. Sometimes the visual and auditory effects of late arrivals and early departures can be minimized via the Web conferencing system.

A PATRON BASE WITHOUT LIMITS OR BORDERS

Often an online library program attracts people from around the globe. However, the majority of the members of a virtual studio audience are in the 48 contiguous United States; therefore, the start time in those four time zones is a key interest. Generally, I have found that programs in the daytime—beginning after 8 A.M. on the West Coast and concluding before 5 P.M. on the East Coast—draw larger audiences than evening programs. However, some types of online programs, such as book discussions, may be more conducive to an evening session. Also, programs held on Tuesday, Wednesday, or Thursday (the core of the typical work week) tend to draw larger virtual studio audiences than online programs held on Friday, Saturday, Sunday, or Monday. This may not be true for your programs and community, so keep statistics and find out what works best, and what doesn't work.

BUILDING A STEADY AUDIENCE

Online programming is a type of experience where, once the user "gets it" (understands it), he or she will likely be very interested in learning about and attending other online programs. Repeat attendees are common, and some attendees could even be labeled voracious. They seem to be charmed by the medium (and its convenience) as much as by the message.

One way to build and maintain a steady audience for an online programming effort is to use the basic concepts of "viral marketing" as discussed in Chapter 6. Encourage attendees to tell their friends and colleagues about your program; and as noted previously, it's always a good idea to remind those receiving e-mail announcements about your programs to forward the message on to anyone who might be interested.

CLASSES AND CLASS CONSCIOUSNESS

Most Web conferencing systems offer different levels of access to tools and control. In essence, each Web conferencing system sets up a class system. In the tcConference Web conferencing system from Talking Communities used by OPAL, users are placed either in the moderator class or the participant class. The power to communicate and to control the communication and behavior of both individuals and groups is not distributed evenly. This class-based situation is not inherently bad or wrong and is found in many other networked computerized information networks, such and online catalogs and blogs, but it must be recognized as what it is. Program hosts and presenters should familiarize themselves before the online event with the way the event will be experienced by regular attendees. Also, if a program host or presenter is going to invoke some system function that is available only to them, it is courteous to explain to regular attendees what you are about to invoke.

PARTICIPATORY PROGRAMMING

The ability of an online programming service and of online library systems and services in general to build a sense of worthwhile participatory online communities of information seekers and learners appears to be a crucial component of the continued growth and success of libraries in the twenty-first century.

One basic decision you want to make about your online program concerns the level of interaction you want both the presenter and the audience to have. At one extreme, an online program can be like a television broadcast. The communication is all one way from the presenter to the attendees, with no real opportunity for real-time feedback, conversation, or other forms of interactivity. At the other extreme, the attendees can have access to all the functionality available to the presenter. In general, the more interaction the audience can engage in, the more involved they will be with the program. If participants can text chat amongst themselves, ask questions and make comments to the presenter (either via text chat or voice-over-IP), and express their opinions via pop up polls, chances are they will view a live synchronous online event as better than both asynchronous online information sharing and in-person events.

Regardless of the type of online programming your library or library consortium offers, there really is no compelling reason not to make it as participatory for attendees as possible. Passive consumption of broadcast programming—just listening to and watching talking heads— is no longer necessary with online programming.

If you think of communication as the confluence of several channels, such as voice-over-IP, video-over-IP, text chatting, presenting slides, and co-browsing, often the text chat channel is a prime time channel for audience participation. People often seem compelled to text chat while they listen and/or watch an online presentation. Sometimes the text chat is in direct response to something being said or shown by the presenter. A few people in the virtual studio audience may text chat off into a tangential topic.

One general mantra of early online programming efforts is to encourage audience involvement and participation. Encourage people to text chat during a live presentation. (As an aside, it appears that the frequency with which one text chats is inversely related to one's age.) The more people get involved, the better their experience will be; and text chat is a great way for your audience to participate.

There are other ways to involve the virtual studio audience in an online programming event. Polls and surveys can be conducted during and after online events to increase the level of audience participation. After the combo live in-person and online battle of the bands that the Johnson County Library in Kansas held during the summer of 2005, the audio files of each band's performance were placed in the OPAL archive along with an option to "vote for your favorite band" of the group. In some elemental way, it is comforting and reassuring to know that the same band that won the in-person one-night competition also won the extended online battle of bands accomplished via the OPAL archive—at least so far.

If you are able to attract a wide variety of people to an online event, there may be a wonderful cross-fertilization of ideas, but there also may be widely divergent expectations across the entire virtual studio audience regarding the content, delivery, and level of audience participation. Recently I attended an online historical lecture that appeared to attract some librarians, some high school instructors, some high school students, and some members of the general public. The high school students engaged in text chatting more than the other demographic groups. Their idea of how to participate in an online event is more akin to a call-and-response mode of audience participation than quietly listening to a presentation. What may appear to be rude behavior to one member of a virtual studio audience may be understood as normal and acceptable, or even positive and responsible, online behavior to another.

In short, online programming has significant potential to help libraries achieve the organizational goal to foster and facilitate more community participation. Encourage attendees to participate, share ideas and opinions, and ask questions. Text chatting, which is available in virtually all Web conferencing systems, is a great channel for audience participation. Pop-up surveys and opinion polls are another great way to encourage audience participation. End-of-event online evaluation forms are a good way to get summative evaluation information from attendees, as well as topical ideas for future online programs. Even users of an archive of recorded online events should be offered ways to interact and develop a sense of community.

I firmly believe that library systems, services, and collections that incorporate this new participatory community spirit will survive and thrive in the new century. This does not mean that one-way, massive, passive broadcasting of information, via such means as television and the traditional methods of publishing a book, will go away. But system designers and managers who truly appreciate the value of usage to the system, whether it is via raw usage reports or through higher order input from users of the system, eventually will become stronger systems.

RIGHTS, PERMISSIONS, AND OTHER INTELLECTUAL PROPERTY MATTERS

Because an online library program is a piece of intellectual property created through the collaborative efforts of many people, you need to, as manager of the online library programming effort, plan for and maintain a set of documents regarding rights, permissions, and other matters pertaining to intellectual property. The right to record an online program and make the recording available on a public Web site must be articulated in some way to all parties involved. Also, adding the presentation slides from an online program may require permission from the creator of those slides.

If your library or library-related organization is planning an online programming service, consider the thorny issues of rights and permissions. Basically you will be broadcasting programs over the Internet, and recordings usually can be made by the event organizers as well as individual members of the virtual studio audience. So, by the conclusion of the online event, there may be multiple copies of the event residing on various hard drives and servers controlled by people who attended the event.

The recording function of the Web conferencing service you select for your online programming service will usually record the audio, the video (if available), the text chatting, the presentation slides displayed, and the Web sites visited. One source of potential trouble here is that generally multiple people input content into the online event being broadcast and recorded. In addition to the presenter(s), any member of the virtual studio audience may say, signal visually, or write something that may be construed as libelous, defamatory, or legally actionable in some other way. Because of this possibility, everyone attending an online event needs to be made aware of the fact that the event is being broadcast, recorded, and/or podcast.

Another thing to be careful about is using copyright-protected information as part of your online event. Examples of this include music that may be played prior to or during the online event, snippets of literary works that are read aloud during the online event, and trademarks or other images included in presentation slides.

For the sake of this brief overview of rights and permissions in this context, let's assume that the library or other organization behind the online programming service is offering the online programs and the recorded programs in the archives free of charge. That way there is no attempt to profit from the recording and distribution of this online programming content. And if we assume that the files containing the archived recorded events are not protected by digital rights management (DRM) in any way, they can and will be copied and shared throughout the world.

Although the rights and permissions issues with free, live, open online programs can become thorny, don't allow your qualms based on flights of imagination about the potential legal issues to result in non-activity in this vital area. When asked if you may record, archive, and podcast an online live event, most presenters and participants immediately grant an enthusiastic positive response. Ideally, permissions to record and disseminate a recording should be in writing. At the very least, include an announcement that the online event is being recorded in the recording itself.

SUSTAINABILITY ISSUES

An online programming effort requires an ongoing, daily commitment. The program Web site, the calendar, program planning and development, promotional efforts, the program archive, and other aspects of the service require frequent, often daily, attention. Burnout of the program coordinator is an area of vulnerability and concern, especially if this person is already overloaded with other responsibilities. Usually the program coordinator will perform a wide variety of tasks related to the program, so boredom born of a narrow set of tasks should not be a problem. Encourage the program coordinator to create a healthy, sustainable mix of tasks the coordinator knows well with new challenges related to the development of the service.

Consistent quality of the online programs and general perceptions of value are essential to sustaining an online programming initiative, too. Although a steadily rising gasoline price is a good incentive for any organization to try Web conferencing, the general experience of the online events offered must be sufficiently satisfactory to ensure repeat and sustained use of the service. The best way to keep the quality high is to evaluate your program routinely, ask participants for their input on future events, and keep making improvements based on the feedback you receive.

COLLABORATIVE OPPORTUNITIES

Although an online library programming effort need not involve the collaboration of two or more libraries to be successful, early experience with this type of programming indicates some advantages to a collaborative effort.

To collaborate or not to collaborate, that is the question. Your library certainly is welcome to investigate and learn from other collaborative programming services, but it is under no obligation to collaborate with anyone in this service area. The calculus of collaboration basically boils down to the following: If your library goes it alone, your library assumes all of the risk, work, and responsibility for the service, as well as the reward. In return, however, your library exercises total control over the service, programmatic directions, and the quality of the online events themselves. If you go it alone, you get all the work, but also all the control. Obviously, the financial burden of developing, launching, and sustaining the online programming service also rests squarely on your library.

If your library decides to go it alone in developing and launching an online programming service, the principal relationship will be between your library and the Web conferencing service you select. If your library decides, on the other hand, to collaborate with other libraries to develop and operate an online programming service, your library will interact with the other libraries involved in the collaborative.

Collaborating on a library programming service means that the costs, labor, and risks are all shared by the participating libraries and library-related organizations. It also means that, by collaborating together, a group of libraries should be able to offer a greater number and wider variety of on-line public programs than most libraries could offer operating alone. The users, not just the organizations, directly benefit from this type of organizational collaboration.

The nuts and bolts of collaboration are beyond the scope of this book, but in brief, a collaborative effort could entail a loose federation of libraries that are collaborating specifically and exclusively for the purposes of the online programming service, or it could involve libraries already involved in an established consortium. Online programming also can lead to new collaborative efforts between existing consortia.

Another advantage of collaborating is to achieve certain economies of scale. For example, during the first official year of the OPAL collaborative service (August 2005 through July 2006), libraries and library-related organizations were able to experiment with Web conferencing software at a very nominal cost. The $200 annual organizational membership dues provided each member library (or group of libraries, because two or more libraries could share one OPAL membership) with a 25-seat "private" room which that OPAL member could schedule and use in any way. The cost per seat per month was only 67 cents. In addition to the private room, OPAL member organizations also had access on a first-come, first-served basis to the larger communal rooms, such as the 200-seat auditorium. First scheduling priority for these communal rooms is for "fully public" programs—programs open to library users worldwide.

Through collaboration the group of collaborating libraries and library organizations are able to offer a wide variety of online programs without placing a huge program development burden on any individual library. The critical mass for a series of online programs—in terms of numbers of programs offered—is still not known, but through collaboration you can usually fill up a schedule quickly.

Another advantage to collaboration in this programmatic area is that it is easier to offer a wide variety of programs, because each collaborating library has its own collection strengths, areas of expertise, mission, and core clientele. If you want to offer programming for children, teens, older adults, and other age groups, a group of libraries working together will probably reach that goal faster than any one library acting unilaterally.

Collaboration among geographically dispersed libraries also helps address the time zone challenges of a global programming effort. We often schedule OPAL programs so that they begin at 2 P.M. Eastern Time, 1 Central, Noon Mountain, and 11 A.M. Pacific. (It is a sad but true fact that we often place the "lunch onus" on residents of the Mountain Time Zone, because it is the least populous of the four time zones in the contiguous 48 states.) This arrangement works fine for the four time zones in the contiguous 48 U.S. states, but is a tad early in Hawaii and Alaska, and it's evening in Europe. This schedule does not work well for live online events in the rest of the world. If a group of collaborating libraries are located on several continents, at least some of the online programs offered will begin at a civilized time on that continent.

Offering online programs in languages other than English is another goal that most online programming services need to face in the future. In general, if multiple libraries collaborate, it will likely be easier to achieve this multi-lingual goal.

The big trade-off of a collaborative online programming initiative is loss of local control. No matter how tightly or loosely the collaborative is structured, in some very tangible ways—that occasionally gall and chafe—each individual institution and each individual member of the individual team defers to the needs and will of the group as a whole. Another trade-off is the competition for prime time slots and scarce resources. Although the Internet is a many splendored thing, bandwidth is a limited resource, and most hosted Web conferencing systems put a limit on the number of virtual seats that can be occupied at any given time.

It should be no surprise to anyone that collaborating with other libraries on anything is not all cakes and ale. It takes dedication, hard work, and patience to sustain a successful collaborative effort. Any collaborative effort entails some risks and downsides.

If a collaborative online programming service asks the member organizations to pay an annual membership fee, the fiscal management challenges may also be significant. Invoicing requirements and payment methods may vary considerably from one library to the next.

Finally, if a collaborative Web conferencing service involves sharing any communal rooms, then the group of libraries will need some method of scheduling the communal rooms so that reservations and the availability of the communal rooms can be quickly ascertained by all, preferably in real time.

FREQUENCY AND SATURATION OF ONLINE PROGRAMS

Eventually all media and event realms must confront the issues of frequency and saturation. Although in the early days of television many stations concluded their "programming day" typically at midnight and resumed it typically at 6 A.M., nearly every television station now has gone to 24/7 broadcasting. The invasion of paid 30- and 60-minute infomercials into the broadcasting days of some television stations—even during normal waking hours—may be troubling, but the stations are still broadcasting something.

There used to be weekly newspapers, and in many metropolitan areas there were both morning and evening newspapers (usually published by different, competing companies), but the daily newspaper now has become the norm.

Likewise, football events used to follow a typical pattern. The high school teams would play on Friday nights, the college teams would play on Saturday afternoons, and the professional teams would play on Sunday afternoons. Now, however, football games are played five or six days each week for nearly half the year. So, event saturation is everywhere.

Online library events are still relatively few and far between, but it is not too early to begin wondering and worrying about online event saturation. The optimal frequency for online programming events remains very much an open question. Some online library programming services seem to be trying to offer as full and varied a schedule of online events as possible, while others seem to be shooting for the once per day, per week, or per month targets.

How much online library programming can a given population find useful and enjoyable? Although saturation questions are more pressing for more established media (such as television) and more established events (such as football games), it is an issue that online programming eventually will need to address. Although online programming does not involve the same time commitment as in-person events, because there is no travel time and time spent waiting for the live event to begin (an attendee can work on other computer-related events while waiting for an online event to begin), there still is a commitment of time and attention, and you'll need to know the limits.

Good online library programs always find and hold an audience. Library vendors, publishers, and other library-related organizations have the promotional savvy and resources to draw respectable to large virtual studio audiences to their online events. These online program providers tend to focus on and adopt the programming philosophy of a relatively small number of online programs that tend to be large online events.

POTENTIAL SOURCES OF COST RECOVERY AND REVENUE

Cost recovery is a key component of the development of a sustainable online programming service. Every online programming effort I know of is trying to figure out sustainable ways to recover its direct costs and to generate a sufficient amount of revenue to develop and enhance the service.

One way for a collaborative online programming effort to generate revenue is to charge the member libraries and organizations an annual membership fee. Even if your library decides to operate an online program unilaterally, it may be possible to generate some revenue through special online events, workshops and mini conferences that generate revenue from registration fees, exhibitor fees, and fees paid for tiered sponsorship levels.

ONLINE PROGRAMMING AS PART OF THE LIBRARY 2.0 MOVEMENT

Do not assume that online programming merely aspires to emulating live in-person library programming. Online programming may evolve rapidly into an entirely different beast altogether.

Instead, proceed with caution as you try to understand Web conferencing systems as a technology that will supplement or replace in-person programs, conferences, and meetings, not to mention conference calls and person-to-person long distance calls. Although your initial understanding of online events may be as in-person events delivered online, the affordances (see Chapter 1) of Web conferencing software may inspire users to move quickly beyond that rather limiting vision.

The big difference between an online programming initiative and other types of Library 2.0 library initiatives, such as blogs, wikis, and vlogs (short video blogs), is that online programming is more direct, immediate, and thus perhaps "warmer" than these other methods of communicating and sharing information. Online programming is live and immediate. There is a palpable sense of a human gathering that you do not get through blogs and wikis.

Although online programming is not as visible or perhaps as important as other technologies currently available, its position and value may rise if some of the basic precepts of the Library 2.0 movement are broadly adopted and diffused through librarianship. If the goal of building communities gains ground on the goal of building collections, the value of online programming may rise, because online programming is an excellent tool in the effort to build and sustain online communities. Gatherings and conversation, whether in a library, in a community, in a bar or pub, or in an online environment, are the building blocks of a sense of community.

In the time being, Web conferencing systems are not often mentioned—and presumably considered—as part of the Library 2.0 toolset. Part of the cause of this general overlook is the historical fact that most Web conferencing systems antedate the articulation and proselytizing of the Library 2.0 movement. When Web conferencing systems were new, most were far too expensive for most libraries and library-related organizations. Now that Web conferencing systems no longer are as new, sexy, and expensive as in years of yore, they often are not considered by librarians as a viable and valuable tool in the Library 2.0 makeover of a library.

CONCLUSION

The key issues raised by using Web conferencing systems to deliver public online programs are invigorating, not enervating. Some of these issues are fundamental to the enterprise and will persist for as long as this type of service persists. Other issues may go away, only to be replaced by new issues. As a manager of an online public programming initiative, you should try to maintain current knowledge about these issues and the concomitant opportunities they present.

11

Into the Future

CHAPTER SUMMARY

The book concludes with speculation, advocacy, and specific recommendations about how online library programming could become a major component of near-term and future full-service digital libraries.

INTRODUCTION

All libraries offer programs to the populations they serve. These programs take many different forms, depending on the population served: story hours, scholarly lectures, retirement seminars, poetry readings, battling bands, gaming events, and more. Although all libraries offer these public programs, most librarians probably would not argue that public programming is one of the absolutely essential activities of any library. Compared to building collections, creating and organizing metadata about information objects, providing reference service, and maintaining networked information systems, public programming seems to be a decidedly second or third tier type of activity—valuable and worthwhile, yes, but not truly essential.

THE VALUE OF PUBLIC PROGRAMMING

The value of public programming, however, in the context of the overall mission of the library may be rising for several reasons. As libraries become more digital and virtual, and as user-contributed metadata become more important to the overall information system, the value of collection development, library-generated metadata, and core public services such as reference may be declining slightly.

As transportation and travel expenses continue what appears to be a steady, inexorable rise, libraries, library-related organizations, and library users will undoubtedly be looking for more cost-effective means to experience provocative live events and engage in lively dialogue with others who are interested in a topic, author, or book. Furthermore, the costs of Web conferencing will probably continue to decline, even as the functionality and reliability continues to improve.

In some ways, five types of group communication are in competition for market share. These five types of meetings, listed in the order in which they developed historically, are

- in-person meetings,
- telephone conference calls,
- video conferences,
- online meetings, and
- meetings in virtual environments.

Ultimately, a given population can attend and stomach only so many group meetings. So, the five types of meetings are involved in a zero-sum game. Although in this book we have concentrated on online meetings using Web conferencing software, we are not asserting or defending that at some point in the future online meetings using Web conferencing software will come to dominate the other four types of meetings. We are only saying that online programming will likely gain in popularity and use. The future for online meetings appears bright.

Of course, in-person meetings have the advantages of historical precedence and the apparent preference of most people. In-person meetings generally are perceived as the richest, deepest type of group meeting, because of all the nonverbal communication that occurs, the informal discussions during breaks, the shared refreshments, and so on. Humans are social animals. We like to congregate and interact. The problem with in-person meetings is that they are expensive and time consuming to attend, because they usually involve traveling some distance for some of the attendees. They also involve removing people from their normal work environments. This can be a positive or negative aspect of in-person meetings, depending on the goals of the meeting and how the attendees react to being removed from their normal routine and work environment. For some people, in-person meetings increase their thoughtfulness and creativity. For others, the change in routine and the excitement of traveling to the in-person event leaves them distracted, unable to concentrate, and susceptible to the lures close to the meeting location, such as local shops, the hotel bar, or the exercise room.

Telephone conference calls have a well-established routine and broad acceptance, but they are struggling to keep up. Many telephone conference call services now offer the ability to record a conference call so they can be archived or shared with those who were unable to participate in the live call. And as long as all or the majority of the people participating in a telephone conference call are near a computer with an Internet connection, it is possible to guide a group of people engaged in a telephone conference call through collaborative browsing.

Although telephone conference calls are not as expensive as in-person meetings, they can still be pricey. Also, the size of a group that can meaningfully interact during a telephone conference call is limited. Having live in-person events that draw in the hundreds or thousands are not unusual, but telephone conference calls cannot accommodate such large numbers without cacophony and chaos ensuing.

Live group meetings in virtual environments may experience significant growth in market share in the coming years and decades even though most virtual environments currently require powerful computers and high bandwidth, and thus cannot be accessed by a high percentage of people.

Online programming is a giant leap toward equalizing access to social and cultural programming for the entire population. Granted, not everyone has ready access to an Internet-connected computer, but an increasing majority of our population does. The percentage of the population with the wherewithal to attend online programming that interests them is much higher than the percentage of the population able to travel (on a regular basis) to in-person events of interest to them.

Online library programming services are still in their infancy, and we do not really know how many months or years it takes for a service to reach maturity. It is probably safe to say that online programming using Web conferencing software has not yet reached its point of maximum of diffusion and use. This is likely true for the general population, and especially true for libraries and library-related organizations. The challenge to increasing the use of Web conferencing software for online events in library and information science is not primarily a technological or economic problem, but rather one of raising awareness of the possibilities and developing social acceptance of this technology within our profession.

Looking into the future of online programming services, we can predict with some certainty an increase in the number of (and attendance to) online programs. Over the next couple of decades we probably will witness a decline in travel to library-sponsored programs, library workshops, and conferences. The situation probably will not be one where online programming pushes in-person programming offstage and into the wings. Rather, the rising costs and perceived inconvenience of travel to attend in-person

workshops, conferences, and lectures will nudge and encourage organizations and individuals to seek out alternatives. The rapid rise of gasoline prices in 2008 gave us a glimpse of the future.

Currently, most online programs emulate the accepted mode of standard
in-person presentations. The speaker speaks while displaying a series of
PowerPoint presentation slides, engages in some Q&A discussion with the
audience, then gets off the stage. As online programs mature and become
more popular, we may start to see different program formats and modes of
interaction emerge. For example, a type of program that merges a general
orientation session with a focus group session could appear. More specifically, a library could provide a general orientation session to a new digital
audio book service; then, when the goals and procedures of the service are
fresh in the minds of the virtual studio audience, the program coordinator
could ask audience members to complete an online interest survey. In some
Web conferencing systems it is very easy to push surveys and polls out to
people in the online room.

Another thing that may change as online programming grows and evolves
is the use of breakout sessions. During in-person programs, workshops, and
conferences, breakout sessions are rather difficult, logistical challenges for
the event organizers. For instance, often people need to get up and move.
Everyone interested in topic X, please go to this table or to this smaller room
down the hall. Everyone interested in topic Y, please move over to this other
corner. It can also be an audio challenge, because without proper facilities,
the sound from one breakout group's discussion can distract the participants
in another breakout session. I have attended conferences where accordion
room dividers are unfurled during a break between a main session and
breakout sessions, but even this isn't always enough.

In online programs, workshops, and conferences, it is much easier to
engage in breakout sessions. All the breakout groups will have access to
the same technology, too.

Technologically, there are very few challenges to be overcome at this
point. The overwhelming majority of libraries and library users now have
Internet-connected computers. Not all of them have broadband connectivity
to the Internet, but that is changing, slowly but surely. The fiscal challenges
are not really substantial. I predict the cost of Web conferencing will continue to decline even as the functionality and reliability continue to improve.

The real challenge, then, is one of adoption and diffusion. It is between
our ears. We need to get more librarians and library users comfortable with
Web conferencing technology and online events.

While one goal in writing this book has been to help readers become
aware of all the options and decision points involved in planning for, launching, and sustaining a useful online programming service, it would be a shame
if you came away feeling overwhelmed, petrified, and overly cautious. The
spirit of agile experimentation is crucial to a viable online programming

service, especially during the rough and tumble early years of this exciting new field of service to the public. The situation will eventually settle down into a routine with a more predictable—or, manageable—set of management challenges. This is to be both expected and rued. Using one's wits and imagination to explore a new area of library service, communication, and community building is as exciting and exhausting as raising children or any other new endeavor. As sixteenth-century English poet Edmund Spenser wrote, "Sleepe after toyle, port after stormie seas, ease after warre, death after life does greatly please" (*The Faerie Queene* [1596]).

WILL MEETINGS IN VIRTUAL WORLDS OVERTAKE WEB CONFERENCING?

The emergence of in-world group events in a virtual world environment is a more recent development than Web conferencing group events. Because avatars serve as in-world representatives, in-world meetings enable the creature interaction and nonverbal communication through body language, gestures, and facial expressions that are common during in-person gatherings but difficult or impossible to convey during group events using telephone conferencing, video conferencing, and Web conferencing. Although meetings in three-dimensional virtual worlds may eventually be generally accepted as the best substitute for in-person meetings, it probably will take several years for the tech bar and user acceptance of virtual world meetings to match where those levels are today for meetings held online via Web conferencing.

WHAT IS THE FUTURE OF ONLINE PUBLIC PROGRAMMING OFFERED BY LIBRARIES?

Programs for the general public seem to be in a transitional phase. Broadcast media, such as television and radio, seem to be losing their grip over the collective attention of the general public. Replacement media, such as YouTube and social networking Web sites, are rapidly gaining in the attention market.

Compared to these global trends and upheavals, the future of public programs offered by libraries may seem inchoate, dim, and definitely small potatoes. Nevertheless, libraries, museums, and other public good institutions have a vital—if small, when measured in the vast market for attention—role to play.

AFTER THE FUN WEARS OFF

One other question we must ask is, Do people who participate in live online events really like online programming in its own right, or do they simply "tolerate" an online event because they are interested in the topic and/or speaker, but do not have the time or travel budget to attend a live in-person event? Is an online event simply a barely tolerable substitute for the "real thing" (a live in-person lecture, workshop, or conference), or is it capable of satisfying on its own in a sustained way the basic human needs that led to the emergence of lectures, workshops, and conferences in the first place? The answer to this question may contain a clue to the overall longevity possibilities for online programming.

Consider the novelty and fun factors of online conferencing. It is one thing to experience a successful online event for the first time and feel the sudden liberation from the need to travel to group meetings, and quite another thing to contemplate sitting in one's office or cubicle day after day, week after week, experiencing a steady stream of online meetings and events. Online library programs may eventually experience a collective psychological backlash and resulting loss of numbers and attention.

At this point in time, it is difficult to determine if live online programs have a certain novelty appeal that eventually will wear off. It has been my observation that there is a certain "ah ha effect" when a person first enters an online event. They suddenly understand the power and usefulness of live online events, and you can almost feel their imaginations begin to churn, thinking of potential uses of such an online meeting space.

CONCLUSION: BACK TO THE FIVE MODES OF SYNCHRONOUS GROUP COMMUNICATION

At this time, of the five basic ways groups can convene and communicate (in-person, via telephone, via video conferencing, online, and in-world), Web conferencing online is the best overall way (in terms of the least expensive, quickest, easiest, most effective, and most "green") for communicating and sharing information among a group. In-person gatherings, however, remain the most comfortable and satisfying of the five modes, although in-person gatherings may not qualify as the platonic ideal of group gatherings and communication. They are inherently expensive in terms of travel costs and time commitment.

Compared to in-person events and telephone conference calls, online events using Web conferencing software, along with video conferencing events and virtual world events, have only a tiny portion of the market share of public and library professional events. It seems safe to predict that Web conferencing-based events will gain market share in the coming years. The usability and usefulness of most Web conferencing systems, coupled with an excellent cost-benefit ratio, almost ensures that Web conferencing will continue to garner more acceptance and use.

References and Resources

Anonymous. 2008. Is it real or is it videoconferencing? *PC Magazine* 27 (1/2) (January): 86.

Anonymous. 2007. Competition between Web-conferencing vendors heats up. *Business Wire*, February 7, 2007. http://findarticles.com/p/articles/mi_m0EIN/is_2007_Feb_7/ai_n27140719/.

Bell, Lori, and Thomas A. Peters. 2004. Online programming can be a library oasis on the Internet. *Computers in Libraries* 24 (10) (November/December): 18–24.

Bell, Stephen, and John D. Shank. 2006. Conferencing @ your computer. *Library Journal* (March 1).

Dickinson, John. 2007. Videoconferencing that works. Finally! *Computerworld* 41 (37) (September 10): 44–48.

Farkas, Meredith. 2007. Learning on a shoestring: Your next conference may be on your desktop. *American Libraries* 38 (9) (October): 45.

Finkelstein, Jonathan. 2006. *Learning in real time: Synchronous teaching and learning online*. San Francisco, CA: Jossey-Bass Wiley.

Heck, Mike. 2005. Web conferencing: It's like being there, virtually—Real-time collaboration services satisfy most meeting needs. *InfoWorld* 27 (19) (May 9, 2005): 12–15. www.infoworld.com/d/developer-world/web-conferencing-its-being-there-virtually-977.

Higgs-Horwell, Melissa, and Jennifer Schwelik. 2007. Building a professional learning community: Getting a large return on a small investment. *Library Media Connection* 26 (3) (November): 36–38.

Houghton-Jan, Sarah. 2008. Online marketing for libraries. Presented online, May 8, 2008. The full streaming playback (audio, slides, text chat) is available at www.opal-online.org/HoughtonJan20080508. The downloadable MP3 audio

recording is available at www.opal-online.org/HoughtonJan20080508/
    HoughtonJan20080508.mp3.

Isakson, Carol. 2005. Caught on the Web. *Education Digest* 70 (7) (March): 79–80.

Middleton, Vanessa D., and Hope Kandel. 2005. Virtual conferencing: Tools to
    achieve global librarianship, professional development, networking and collabo-
    ration. In *Electronic information resources in the Caribbean*, 137–38. University
    of the West Indies.

Murray, Charles J. 2007. A new era of video conferencing. *Design News* 62 (15)
    (October 22): 64–68.

Perez, Ernest. 2004. Web conferencing for libraries: Can you hear me now? *On-
    line* 28 (1) (January–February): 29–31. www.infotoday.com/online/jan04/
    perez.shtml.

Peters, Tom, and Lori Bell. 2006. Is Web conferencing software ready for the big
    time? *Computers In Libraries* 26 (2): 32–35.

Raunik, Anna. 2006. An investigation of streaming—Webcasting and Webconfer-
    encing technologies in the US and UK. www.valaconf.org.au/vala2006/
    papers2006/100_Raunik_Final.pdf (accessed October 14, 2007).

Raunik, Anna. 2006. Streaming live from libraries . . . *incite* 27 (3): 14.

Smith, Kelly A. 2006. The virtual viewpoint. *Serials Review* 32 (3): 195–203.

Survey of online meeting tools. Presented by Publicare. www.webconferencing-test
    .com (accessed October 19, 2008).

Index

SirsiDynix Institute, 43, 122

talking communities, 19, 41–2, 52, 66, 77, 122, 139
technical support, 56, 73–74
telepresence technologies, 9–10
text chat, 4, 46, 64–65, 75; private, 75; recording, 113
time-shifting, 110
training sessions, 36, 81–86; goals of, 83–84

URLearning (*Library Journal*), 43, 96
usage reports, 72, 78–79, 96; of an archive of recordings, 116–17

VCL MIG (Virtual Communities and Libraries, Member Initiative Group, of the American Library Association), 11
video conferencing, 8–9
video-over-IP, 66, 76
viral marketing, 93

virtual worlds, 9–10, 153. *See also* MUVE
VoIP (voice-over-Internet Protocol), 3–4, 65, 75

Web 2.0. *See* Library 2.0
Web conferencing, 9, 15
Web conferencing software, 52, 60–61; arguments against, 129–30; evaluation of, 120–21; recording features, 110–11; reliability of, 73; selection criteria, 63–64; underutilization of by libraries, 127–28
WebJunction Wimba, 43–44
Web server logs. *See* usage reports
Web sites supporting online programs, 55–56, 92
whiteboards, 70, 76
Wiki defined, 2
wisdom of crowds, 3
workshops, 100–101

YouTube, 94

About the Author

THOMAS A. PETERS is the founder, CEO, and Grand Poobah of TAP Information Services (www.tapinformation.com), which helps organizations innovate. He is the coordinator of OPAL (www.opal-online.org) and of Unabridged (www.unabridged.info), a downloadable digital audio book service for blind and low-vision readers.